Betty Crocker

WIN AT WEIGHT LOSS COOKBOOK

A Healthy Guide for the Whole Family

WILEY

Wiley Publishing, Inc.

This book is dedicated to my family, Trish, Alex and Michael, who have been wonderful in putting up with me and all of the the time I spend away from home, promoting the small changes message. Thanks for your love and support.

Library of Congress Cataloging-in-Publication Data:

Crocker, Betty.

  [Win at weight loss cookbook]

  Betty Crocker win at weight loss cookbook : a healthy guide for the whole family / Betty Crocker.

     p. cm.

  Includes index.

  ISBN-13: 978-0-7645-9610-0 (cloth)

  ISBN-10: 0-7645-9610-1 (cloth)

  1. Reducing diets—Recipes. 2. Children—Nutrition. 3. Family—Nutrition. I. Title.

RM222.2.C7493 2006

641.5'635--dc22

                                2005024916

Manufactured in the United States of America.

10 9 8 7 6 5 4 3 2 1

Title page image © 2005 Dennis Harms c/o theispot.com

General Mills, Inc.

Director, Book and Online Publishing: Kim Walter

Manager, Cookbook Publishing: Lois Tlusty

Editor: Cheri Olerud

Recipe Development and Testing: Betty Crocker Kitchens

Photography and Food Styling: General Mills Photography Studios

Wiley Publishing, Inc.

Publisher: Natalie Chapman

Executive Editor: Anne Ficklen

Senior Production Editor: Michael Olivo

Cover Design: Fritz Metsch and Susan Alfieri

Interior Design and Layout: Mauna Eichner and Lee Fukui

Manufacturing Manager: Kevin Watt

Thanks go to:

- Joyce Hendley for her outstanding writing
- Bell Institute of Health and Nutrition members Sarah Olson and Jean Storlie
- A heartfelt thanks to the following families who provided insightful quotes and shared the things that have worked for them in their quest to become more active and maintain their weight: Deb M., Alyson S., Greg S., Clarke S., North S., Elizabeth H., Steve, Cheri, Christian, Carlon and Ruby O.

Our Betty Crocker Kitchens seal guarantees success in your kitchen. Every recipe has been tested in America's Most Trusted Kitchens™ to meet our high standards of reliability, easy preparation and great taste.

Find more great ideas and shop for name-brand housewares at

BettyCrocker.com

* * *

Want to make a powerful start on a family weight loss journey? In this cookbook, you'll find the tools you'll need to help you succeed together, beginning with the discovery that *a child's family is one of the most powerful influences on his or her weight and health*.

This book shows you the small, simple steps you can take to strengthen the foundations of a healthy lifestyle. *Parents and caretakers are a child's most important role models* and the family home is a powerful place to develop lifelong healthy habits. The relationships families develop around food, physical activity and each other play a key role in shaping children's health, both now and for years to come.

This approach focuses on making exercise an easy and fun family habit. As children become more active, they can "grow into" a healthier weight. Tips on nutrition, food and activity at each stage of your child's growth and development are also included, beginning at age 3.

Maintaining a healthy weight benefits every family member and can help reduce the chance of developing cancer, diabetes and heart disease. You'll all look better, feel better and have more energy. Of greatest importance, you'll be passing along a positive, lasting lifestyle to your children.

So, turn the page and come on, start winning at the weight loss game!

James O. Hill

Dr. James O. Hill

contents

THE WEIGHT LOSS GAME: IT'S A FAMILY AFFAIR

"I really try to get my children to eat healthy food and exercise, but all they want to do is eat fast food and watch TV. What can I do?"

"I heard kids are getting fatter because portion sizes are getting bigger. Is this true — and if so, what can we do about it?"

"I try to provide healthy food at home, but my kids are hardly ever around. I have little control over what they eat when they're at school, friends' houses or out in the community. What can I do?"

"All of us in the family—kids and parents— are overweight. We have so much weight to lose it seems hopeless. Why bother?"

If you're one of the many people who have asked themselves questions like these, you'll find real help in these pages. Just by coming here, you've made a powerful start on a family weight loss journey—and you'll find the tools you need to help you succeed together.

If a health care professional has advised someone in your family to lose weight, you have lots of company: At last count, nearly two-thirds of American adults had extra pounds to lose. More troubling is the finding that today, nearly a third of all American children are either overweight, or at risk of becoming so. This increases their risks of developing heart disease, diabetes and other conditions related to excess weight—and, in a society that prizes thinness, challenges their self-esteem.

Compounding the problem, overweight kids are more likely to carry their excess weight into adulthood, especially if their parents also have weight problems. In fact, overweight and obesity tend to run in families, and kids are much more likely to be overweight if one or both of their parents are, too.

But turn those statistics around, and you'll discover the good news: *A child's family is one of the most powerful influences on his or her weight and health.* Harness that "family power" to build healthy eating and exercise habits together, and your chances of success are strong indeed! Just as a team beats a single player in tug-of-war, a family is more likely to reach its goals than a child, teen or adult "going it alone" in the weight loss game.

The Game Plan

This book focuses on the simple steps you can take as a family to build and strengthen the foundations of a healthy lifestyle, together. At its core is the understanding that parents and caretakers are children's most important role models—and that the family home is a powerful training ground for lifelong habits. The healthy relationships families develop around food, physical activity and each other play a key role in shaping children's beliefs and behaviors—and, ultimately, their health. Rather than recommending restrictive diets (which are inappropriate for most children), this approach centers on helping children become more active with the support of their families, so that they may "grow into" a healthier weight.

This section begins with some basic principles of healthy eating. Next, you'll find a discussion of nutrition and activity issues at each stage of your child's growth and development. There are practical guidelines for making exercise a fun family habit, no matter how active your family is now—and tips for stocking a healthy kitchen. Then, you'll find the easy, family-friendly recipes to help put those recommendations into practice, deliciously. And, they are all appropriate for the "family team" to cook together!

Not All Foods Are Created Equal

The fuel your body needs comes from calories, but not all foods are created equal. Gram for gram, some foods are more concentrated sources of calories than others.

Eating more calories than your body needs as fuel—whether they come from carbohydrates, protein or fat—will be stored as fat, resulting in weight gain.

Energy Source	Calories per Gram
Fat	9 calories per gram
Protein	4 calories per gram
Carbohydrates	4 calories per gram

One of the basic guidelines for good health is to maintain a healthy weight. That can be easier said than done, but the key to weight management has always involved three basic steps: *balanced eating, calorie control* and *exercise.* The bottom line? "Calories in" must equal "calories out," and a calorie is a calorie, whether it comes from fat, protein or carbohydrates. To lose weight, you need to eat fewer calories and exercise more.

Q. *"My twelve-year-old daughter is overweight. Should I put her on a diet?"*

A. If you think your daughter is overweight, discuss it with her doctor first (and not while she's in the room). Most experts agree that diets requiring severe restriction of food intake are inappropriate for children, unless they've been recommended by a doctor and are conducted under professional supervision. Because children's bodies are still growing, restricting what they eat—especially at ages six and younger—can put them at risk of missing out on nutrients their bodies need.

Rather than put your daughter on a diet, try to help her reduce the rate at which she is gaining weight. That way, she will grow into a healthier weight over time. The good news is that you can do this with some small lifestyle changes.

Start by helping your daughter become more physically active. You might want to encourage her to participate in a sport such as recreational soccer— where kids are at all different skill levels, and where she will run a lot. Or you could just encourage her to walk more; walking is a great form of physical activity. Of course, kids usually do better when parents are active with them—so think about getting in the habit of taking a family walk after dinner or on weekends, or just kicking the soccer ball back and forth around the yard. And, to make sure your daughter has enough "active" time, set some limits on the time she spends watching TV or videos, or on the computer or phone. Throughout this chapter and in the "Resources" section, page 244, you'll find lots of other ideas for helping your child, and the whole family, move more.

On the food side, make sure the foods you keep around the house are those you want your daughter to eat. Like all kids, she'll need snacks, so make sure to have healthier options on hand. Pay particular attention to portion sizes, since large helpings encourage overeating. If you're concerned that she's overeating at school, encourage her to bring along a healthy lunch you've packed—or better yet, have her make it herself, choosing from foods you've provided. View this as an opportunity for her to learn about life-long good food habits.

Finally, after you make these small changes, be patient. You should see your daughter's weight improving, but it will take some time.

The Training Table: Basics of Healthy Eating

What's a healthy diet for kids? For teens? For adults? Although nutritional needs change with age, and dietary recommendations from various health authorities can differ slightly, there are a few key principles of healthy eating that apply to just about everyone of any age: Balance, Variety and Moderation.

Balance the foods you eat with the amount of activity you get each day. If you're moving around a lot, you'll get to eat more than if you're a couch potato.

Try to eat a variety of different foods over the day, and over the course of a week. You can't get all the nutrients you need from just one food, or one type of food (and who could enjoy such a boring diet for long?).

Aim for moderation in your portion sizes and in the quantities of food you eat daily. The goal is to feel satisfied, not stuffed. All foods can fit into a healthy eating pattern, if they're eaten in moderate amounts and balanced with other food choices.

In addition, the "Dietary Guidelines for Americans 2005," issued by the USDA, recommend that you:

- Choose foods that provide adequate nutrients within your calorie needs and limit the amount of saturated and trans fats, cholesterol, added sugars, salt and alcohol.

- Maintain body weight in a healthy range and prevent gradual weight gain over time.

- Engage in at least 30 to 60 minutes of regular physical exercise daily to promote health, psychological well-being and a healthy body weight.

- Foods to eat more of every day:

  - fruits and vegetables—at least 5

  - whole-grain products—at least 3

  - fat-free milk or equivalent milk products— at least 3 cups

Foods to eat less of:

- Fats—keep the amount of fat you consume to 20 to 35% of total calories and cholesterol to 300 mg or less. Eat less than 10% of calories from saturated fatty acids.

- Use liquid oils (like canola or olive oil) rather than solid fat whenever possible.

Eat less than 2,300 milligrams of sodium (about 1 teaspoon of salt) per day and choose foods that contain little salt.

The Powerful Food Pyramid

Most of us well know the time-proven principles, but putting them into practice in our daily lives—and our children's—is more challenging. Is there any such thing as "moderation" at an all-you-can-eat buffet restaurant? Is it possible to get "variety" when your four-year-old will only eat yogurt? That's where the Food Guide Pyramid comes in.

In April 2005, The "My Pyramid Food Guidance System" was introduced. It illustrates healthy eating and reflects the "2005 Dietary Guidelines for Americans" (page 13). The new pyramid emphasizes physical activity, calories and focuses on making smart food choices in every food group, every day.

- Grains: Make half of your grains whole.

- Vegetables: Eat a variety of veggies.

- Fruits: Focus on fruits.

- Milk: Include milk and milk-rich foods.

- Meat and beans: Go lean with protein.

To help Americans build a healthy lifestyle, "My Pyramid" shows:

- Personal recommendations on types and amounts of food to eat each day based on age, gender and activity level.

- Gradual improvement helping people benefit from taking small steps to improve diet and lifestyle.

Emotional Eating

If you have an urgent desire for pizza after a mentally draining day at work, your hunger is likely triggered by emotions. Emotional eating is the urge to eat to satisfy a *feeling* rather than physical hunger. Our bodies give us gradual physiological cues—such as a sense of emptiness, lightheadedness or low energy—when it's time to eat. But emotional hunger can be sudden and specific.

Common triggers for emotional hunger include stress, depression, sadness, anger, loneliness, boredom and fatigue. Using food to alleviate these feelings might make you feel better short term, but doesn't fix the underlying issue.

Emotional eating adds calories your body may not need and can cause you to feel badly about yourself later.

So, before you eat, take the hunger test. Are you really hungry, or just:

bored

angry

sad

lonely

tired (either physically or emotionally)

For more on Emotional Eating, see page 138.

- Physical activity: A person climbing stairs is a graphic reminder to be physically active every day.

- Variety: the six color bands represent the food groups. Foods from all groups are needed each day for good health.

- Moderation: This is represented by the narrowing of each food group from bottom to top.

- Proportionality: This is shown by the different widths of the food group.

MyPyramid.gov
STEPS TO A HEALTHIER YOU

MyPyramid.gov offers Americans a personalized approach to a healthier lifestyle with interactive activities that balance nutrition and exercise. For a tailor-made program for you and your family, go to the Web site: http://mypyramid.gov.

While it's important to be aware of daily requirements, don't forget that the Pyramid is a guideline, not a mandate. It gives helpful goals to shoot for, but what really matters, healthwise, is what we eat over the course of a few days or a week. This is an especially important consideration with children, as their eating can vary widely from day to day, and with their growth patterns. Maybe your four-year-old will only eat a bagel today, but chances are he'll eat other foods tomorrow, as his natural instincts for variety—and his hunger—take over.

Bottom line: Serve foods from each part of the Food Guide Pyramid daily, using the suggested portion sizes as a guide. Don't worry if your child doesn't eat every food group every day; what matters most is that you've made those foods available. Most importantly, make sure you're following the Pyramid guidelines yourself, so that you set a good example. Those actions will "speak" more loudly than anything you say!

Winning Strategies

Now that you know some general guidelines, here are some proven ways to steer the whole family toward better eating habits.

Let kids make choices, within reason. What works best for most families is to offer a range of healthy foods, and let kids decide themselves what they'll take (see "The Healthy Family Pantry," pages 36–38, for ideas). When parents make all the decisions, kids don't learn those skills for themselves—and become less confident of their own abilities. Show them that you trust them to eat well, and they will.

Welcome all foods, in moderation. All foods can be part of a healthy eating pattern, even food like candy or French fries. The key is to enjoy them in moderate amounts, making sure to eat a wide variety of other foods. While this concept seems simple, it's one of the most important eating skills you can teach your child. What's less effective, say experts, is making certain foods off-limits—for example, forbidding your child to eat candy. Studies show that this strategy usually backfires, because it can make kids want the "forbidden" foods even more. By contrast, when you allow occasional treats and serve them without fanfare, you're teaching your child how to approach these foods wisely.

Snacks are okay. Children have small stomachs that need to be refilled more often than adults, so they might not always stay "fueled up" with a traditional three-daily meal pattern. They're likely to have an appetite in between, and snacks can help. The problem lies in making snacks a free-for-all opportunity for "treats" that are high in calories and fat. Think of snacks as mini meals, and approach them in the same way you'd plan breakfast, lunch or dinner—only on a smaller scale. You'll find easy and delicious snack recipes later on in this book; starter suggestions include cut-up raw vegetables with creamy salad dressing "dip," yogurt and fruit, peanut butter spread on whole-grain crackers or apple wedges, or even a half-sandwich. Don't worry if your child eats less at a main meal if she's had a snack; her appetite is simply working the way it should, by preventing her from eating more than she needs.

Provide structured meals. Try to establish regular times for serving meals and snacks, rather than keeping the kitchen open 24/7. Some families find it helpful to make snacks off-limits an hour before meals are served, so that the kids come to the table with an appetite. Meals eaten away from home need structure, too: Children today are faced with daylong "eating opportunities," from snacks designed to be eaten in cars or strollers, to doughnuts regularly served after church, to snacks served after every recreational activity your child is involved in. Setting clear limits and sticking to them, such as saying "choose just one treat from the dessert table," or "no snacking in the car," will help your child develop the skills to resist these all-day temptations.

Get your rest. You may wonder what this has to do with the foods you select and serve to your family, but when we feel tired and run-down, it seems like a much harder task to select and cook good-for-you recipes, stock a healthy pantry, and be active with the kids than it really is. And when you're tired, you may not be as likely to make good food choices: it's much easier to reach for higher-fat convenience foods than cooking a meal.

Stealthy Healthy Cooking

Trying to cut the calories in the foods your family eats? With the wide variety of tasty, reduced-calorie foods available these days, it's easier than ever. A great way to start is to focus on cutting the fat content of the foods you prepare and serve. Since fat contains more than twice the calories as the other types of food we eat, protein and carbohydrates, cutting fat gives you the biggest calorie "bang for the buck." Small changes in fat content will make a big difference in calorie content—and chances are, no one will notice.

Switch to lower-fat dairy products like 1 percent and fat-free milk, cottage cheeses and yogurts; experiment with reduced-fat cheeses, spreads, lunchmeats and salad dressings. Trim the skin off poultry, and choose lean cuts of meat (such as those labeled "loin"); broil foods or stir-fry them in just a little oil, rather than frying them. Keep portion sizes reasonable, so you don't encourage overeating.

You can also cut calories almost without notice by serving foods with a higher water content, such as soups and stews, fruits and vegetables, and cooked grains. Research shows that people tend to eat the same weight of food each day, regardless of calories—and that those "watery" foods tend to weigh more, but have fewer calories, than others. You can pump up the volume of your family's meals by adding extra vegetables to casseroles, stews and pasta dishes, serving fresh fruit for dessert or snacks, and making salad (with low-fat dressing) a regular feature on the family table. All these techniques, and more, can be found in the family-friendly recipes that follow.

Ask Dr. Hill:

Q. *"I heard kids are getting fatter because portion sizes are getting bigger. Is this true — and if so, what can we do about it?"*

A. As Americans are eating more foods from restaurants, take-out stores and other "away-from-home" venues, we've become used to ever-increasing portion sizes. According to a recent study, most marketplace food portions are much bigger than standard portions—sometimes two to eight times larger. This "portion distortion" has caused us to lose touch with what a serving looks like.

Bigger portions have also helped turn many of us into bigger eaters. Studies show that when people are served larger amounts of food, they're more likely to eat more—often without noticing. One study of preschoolers found that when children were repeatedly served lunch portions that were two times normal size, they ate significantly more food, and wolfed it down in larger bites.

Compounding the problem, many of us tend to serve overly generous portions on our own dining tables, too. That teaches our children to think that large portions are the norm, especially if they see their parents loading up their plates.

Learn to Recognize Portion Sizes

What do sensible portions look like? Most are probably smaller than you'd think! To start, make an effort to measure your portions; soon you'll be able to "eyeball" them accurately.

- **Use** familiar objects to help you visualize. Here's a handy chart to guide you:

  3-ounce serving of meat or poultry = About the size of a deck of cards or a cassette tape

  1-ounce cube of cheese = About the size of your thumb or 2 dominoes

  1 teaspoon = About the size of your fingertip (tip to middle joint)

  1 tablespoon = About the size of your thumb tip (tip to middle joint)

  1/2 cup = A fruit or vegetable that fits into the palm of your hand—about the size of a tennis ball

  1 ounce nuts = Fits into the cupped palm of a child's hand

  1 cup = About the size of a woman's fist; cereal that fills half of a standard cereal bowl.

- **Teach** yourself how much your favorite utensils hold, so that you know much "one ladleful" of soup, for example, actually contains. Just fill the utensil with water, then pour the water out into a measuring cup.

- **Get used to** what a portion looks like in a particular bowl or plate—say, a one-half cup serving of cereal in a bowl—then use that same bowl every time you serve that cereal.

- **Recheck** your portion sizes every once in a while. They have a tendency to "creep up" again over time.

Combating Portion Distortion

The best way to combat portion distortion is to learn to recognize what healthy portion sizes look like, focusing on the foods your family eats most often. Then, make an effort to serve and eat realistically portioned meals. In restaurants, be a good role model by sharing an overly large dish—or eating a sensible portion of what you're served, and having the rest wrapped up in a doggy bag. (Ask for the bag right when you're served, so you won't be tempted to eat more than a comfortable amount.)

Kids in the Kitchen

If you'd like your kids to eat better, how about letting them do some of the cooking? Chances are, they'll be eager to help.

When the Betty Crocker Kitchens polled one thousand kids between the ages of ten and seventeen, most (around 80 percent) agreed with the statements "I think cooking is fun," and "I'd like to learn more about how to cook." Nearly two-thirds added that they'd "like to help more with the cooking in my home."

More reasons to open the kitchen doors: When kids have a hand in food preparation, they're more likely to try what's on the menu. That can come in handy if you have picky eaters in your family. And, by giving kids some input on what goes on the family table, you send the message that you trust them to make good decisions about food for the whole family. They'll feel a sense of accomplishment, knowing that their contributions to the family are needed and valued. They also just might discover a terrific new dish!

Where to start? Find an age-appropriate task for your child to help prepare tonight's dinner. Many of the recipes in this book are easy for children to prepare or at least help prepare. Even a three-year-old can help wash vegetables or tear salad leaves; a five-year-old may be able to put out silverware or set the table. A ten-year-old can handle some vegetable chopping, and even some cooking or baking. You might also let the kids plan the menu one night a week (and, depending on their age, prepare it themselves). Enlist their help planning meals, writing a shopping list, buying groceries or tending a family vegetable garden.

The Rules of the Game

Winning the family weight loss game requires that all the players understand a few ground rules: the positions they and the rest of the team play, the extent of their powers, and, most importantly, the strategies that work best with their team's abilities. In this section, we'll review the roles and dynamics of the family team, and how you can make them work in your favor for weight loss success.

Coaches' Corner: Parents as Role Models

Parents and caretakers wear many hats: cooks, chauffeurs, wound-bandagers, bedtime story–readers, homework helpers. But the most important hat is the one that reads "role model." As their children's first teachers, parents' own behavior shapes their children's eating and activity habits.

Right from birth, a child's view of the world begins with what goes on in his own home, and that family's daily routines are what he perceives as "normal." If he sees the adults in his life eating healthy and being active, he'll come to understand that he can do these things, too. On the other hand, if those adults spend all their free time in front of the TV, eating fast food regularly, or drinking soda with dinner instead of milk, they'll have a hard time convincing their children to do otherwise. If they're not "walking the walk," it's not likely their children will listen to their "talk."

So, before you focus on changing your child's eating and activity habits, be sure to review your own, and make changes if you need to. By eating a variety of foods in sensible portions and fitting regular activity into your days, you'll set a good example for your child—and feel better and healthier yourself! Don't worry if your habits haven't been perfect in the past (whose have?), and don't require perfection from yourself, either. It's easier if you start with small changes that you can fit into your busy lives. No matter where you stand now, taking the initiative to make positive changes in your life sends a powerful message to your children that they can do it, too!

The Positive Coach

Many of us have a critical image of our own bodies—especially if we have some weight to lose. How often have you heard yourself say things like, "I'm too fat!" or "my legs are too heavy?" Such "negative self-talk" can affect your child's self-image, too. By criticizing your body, you send the message that your self-worth depends on your weight. Make the effort to refrain from disparaging your body, and that of others, in front of your child. Although it can be a hard habit to break, it can go a long way toward building your child's self-esteem.

The Players' Positions

When it comes to family eating habits, it's helpful to think of parents and children as playing different positions on the team, each with different responsibilities. Recognizing the following division of responsibility, says family nutrition expert Ellyn Satter, RD, is "the golden rule for parenting with food":

- Parents are responsible for what foods go on the table, and how they're presented.

- Children are responsible for what, how much and even whether they eat.

Eating problems develop, says Satter and other experts, if parents don't acknowledge this division of responsibility. It's easy to do, since parents are programmed to want their kids to eat nutritiously and well.

Power Plays

Is the family table a pleasant place to be—or a battleground for power struggles? Perhaps your child won't try a new food you've spent all day preparing, or he balks if the peas on his plate "touched" his spaghetti (more about picky eaters later). Maybe he won't eat anything green—or says he's not hungry, until dessert arrives. What all these situations have in common is that food has become a weapon of power rather than just a nutritional necessity. And the best way to stop these power struggles, research shows, is to take that power away from the food.

Although it takes a good deal of persistence, you can refuse to make food an issue in your household. When a child rejects a food, don't let on that you're disappointed, or make him feel guilty. Just let him choose what he wants from what's on the table, without making an issue of it.

Similarly, if you're serving dessert, don't prevent your child from having some, even if he hasn't eaten as much dinner as you'd like. You could even let him eat dessert first, if that's what he really wants. If you don't let dessert have all-important status in the meal, it will eventually lose its allure.

Inborn Talents

We're all born with an innate ability to sense when we're hungry, and when we're full. Just picture a baby who cries when she needs feeding, and closes her mouth to the spoon when she's had enough cereal. Most young children, too, have a remarkable way of eating just the amount of food they need, and no more. This can drive their parents crazy, since kids' calorie needs can vary widely from day to day!

But as they get older, many children start to rely less on their own hunger and fullness to decide how much they'll eat. Instead, they come to depend more on other cues, like the time of day ("it's noon, so I have to eat lunch") or social obligations ("if I don't eat this, it will go to waste").

Many experts believe that eating problems begin when kids lose touch with those hunger and fullness signals. Once that connection is lost, it's easy for kids to eat even if they're not hungry, or continue eating even after they're full—setting them up for a lifetime of overeating. That's one reason why dieting—which encourages people to ignore hunger pangs—can be problematic for kids in the long term.

Parents can play a powerful role in this loss of appetite-regulating skills. By encouraging a child to eat even when she's not hungry, or urging her to clean her plate before she can leave the dinner table, you send the message not to trust her own instincts.

But parents can also be part of the solution, too. Make an effort to respect your child's appetite by providing her with food when she's hungry, but letting her decide when she's full. That means banishing the "clean plate club" from your house. If you can't bear to see uneaten food go to waste, serve smaller portions and let your child have seconds if she's still hungry.

Don't despair if your child—or you—has already lost touch with hunger and fullness cues. Research suggests that those abilities can be "reawakened" by making an effort to listen to the body's signals. In one study of preschoolers, kids who were given regular sessions of body-awareness exercises (rating their feelings of hunger before, during and after a meal, for example) were better able to regulate their eating, stopping when they'd had enough.

Family Dinner: A Child's Hole in One

One of the most powerful things you can do for your child's health is as simple, and delicious, as sitting down to dinner together. A survey of over 16,000 children found that those who sat down to regular meals with their families tended to eat more fruits, vegetables and nutrients like calcium, iron and fiber. They also tended to eat less fried food, saturated fat and trans fat, and drank fewer sodas.

Other studies show that kids in households with regular family meals tend to score higher in measures of good health, including academic achievement and psychological adjustment. They're also less likely to report behavioral problems and suicidal thoughts, along with alcohol or drug use.

Why do family dinners matter so much? The regular ritual of togetherness helps bolster children's sense of themselves as part of a family community, reinforcing their self-esteem. What's more, carving out time for dinner-table conversation can improve family communication and relationships. This holds true regardless if children are eager toddlers, busy school-agers, or even teens in the "my-parents-are-so-lame" stage. In fact, a Betty Crocker Kitchens survey found that 94 percent of pre-teens and teens agreed with the statement "I like it when my whole family eats together."

But these days, finding time to sit down together seems harder than ever, with dual-career juggling, kids' sports and after-school activities often pre-empting family time. William J. Doherty, Ph.D., Director of the Marriage and Family Therapy Program at the University of Minnesota, recommends the following strategies for reclaiming this endangered family ritual:

Schedule meals. Review the family's schedules to find a few times a week that everyone can share a meal. If it's impossible, consider dropping or curtailing some activities.

Be flexible. It doesn't always have to be dinner; many families find breakfasts work best, or weekend brunch. Take-out food or restaurant meals count, too. How about designating Thursday nights as "pizza night" at your family's favorite pizza parlor?

Give everybody a role. Make it easier on the cook by letting all members pitch in on the family dinner effort. Menu planning, shopping, preparing, setting the table and cleaning up can all be delegated, depending on age and interest. (And, count on kids being interested: in the Betty Crocker Kitchens survey, over two-thirds of kids said they'd be willing to do some of the cooking "if it helped my family to be able to eat dinner together.")

Minimize distractions. Turn off the TV and let the answering machine take your phone calls. Instead, concentrate on each other—and send the powerful message to your children that family matters most.

Ask Dr. Hill:

Q. *"I really try to get my children to eat healthy food and exercise, but all they want to do is eat fast food and watch TV. What can I do?"*

A. There's no doubt that television and fast food are powerful lures. But your powers as a parent to control these outside influences can be just as potent. Focus on limiting, rather than forbidding, these diversions, and giving kids choices within those boundaries. That is, if your kids are restricted to one hour of TV time daily, let them pick the shows they want to watch (with your approval). And, if the family rule is one fast-food meal a week, let the kids decide what they're going to order.

Lastly, don't forget to offer lots of healthy alternatives. Instead of the local burger joint, offer home-cooked meals your kids enjoy, letting them choose from a selection of healthy foods. Continue to set a good example by staying active yourself, and provide your kids with plenty of opportunities to move their bodies.

This section focuses on some of the key stages in your child's development, beginning at around age three, when he or she has likely mastered walking, self-feeding, talking and other milestones of growing independence. (For guidelines regarding younger children and infants, check with your health professional.)

Age 3–5:
The Discoverer

Developmental Insights:

She learns by exploring and questioning her environment—and is beginning to categorize and label what she sees. Her curious mind is ready to absorb simple facts about foods and nutrition. She's learning to use her growing muscles and, with every move, becomes more coordinated and graceful. Her growth rate will begin to level off, with occasional growth spurts. Her appetite will vary with her growth pattern, so don't worry if she doesn't eat the same amounts each day. She might still need an afternoon nap, which shouldn't be skipped. Not getting enough sleep may make her too tired to get the activity she needs (and may increase her risk of becoming overweight).

Parent Tip-offs—Food and Eating:

She has (or will soon) mastered feeding herself, but still needs you to:

- Cut foods into manageable portions.

- Provide a variety of foods, tastes and textures for her to try, in a nonpressured, cheerful environment. It's okay if she plays with her food . . . or says "no!"

- Make certain her food portions are child-size. "The Discoverer" learns visually, so she is building an image of what a "serving" should be.

- Keep fruit juice intake moderate—no more than 6 ozs per day, preferably 100 percent fruit juice products. When she's thirsty, start her on a healthy habit by giving her water, nature's best thirst-quencher.

- Engage her in simple, safe cooking activities, such as washing baby carrots or grapes in a bowl of water. You can also let her watch while you explain what you are doing and why.

Parent Tip-offs—Activity:

- Provide plenty of safe places to play, climb and explore.

- Build a family habit of daily play: explore playgrounds (indoor and outdoor), walking paths, neighborhood parks and pools. Get into the habit of a

Family Challenge: Trying New Foods

Does your child refuse to try new foods? This complaint is so common there's even a scientific term to label it: neophobia, or "fear of the new." It's a fact of life that almost all toddlers or pre-schoolers go through a neophobic stage; such instincts may have once served them well in the hunter-gatherer era, when trying a new food in the wild might have exposed them to poisons. Some kids remain neophobic long past their toddler years, particularly if they are prone to anxiety. But chances are, your child's neophobia will pass eventually, so take heart!

Studies show that the best response to neophobia is patience—and persistence. Children often need to be exposed to a food several times before they'll give it a try—sometimes as many as ten to fifteen times! Offer a new food in a friendly, nonjudgmental way and, if it is rejected, don't make it an issue. Try offering that same food again, after a comfortable interval—say, a week or two. If she does eventually take a bite, don't lavish her with praise, either; one study found that when children were rewarded for trying a new food, they were less likely to eat it again on another occasion. All that encouragement might have made them suspicious!

Other techniques:

- Try new foods that are similar to ones she already likes. If she likes cooked carrots, she might readily try sweet potatoes, for example—or, if she's a peanut butter sandwich fan, she might also enjoy hummus spread on a piece of pita bread, or if she's a cheese sandwich fan, she might also enjoy Three-Cheese and Bacon Spread, page 80, on whole wheat crackers or on a piece of pita bread. Susan B. Roberts, Ph.D., Professor of Nutrition at Tufts University, calls this "building a bridge of familiarity" to new foods.

- Make sure your child is hungry when she comes to the table. If she snacks all afternoon, she won't have an appetite, and will be less likely to accept a new food.

- Don't label her a "picky eater." Your words can shape her expectations of herself—and she'll live up (or down) to them.

family walk after dinner—in fact, why not start a tradition of after-dinner walks?

- Encourage her to get out and do some of the walking herself if you're still using a stroller.

- Keep her on a regular sleep schedule, including a nap if she needs one.

Age 6–10:
The Independent

Developmental Insights:

His growth is slower and steadier, allowing him to build more physical skills. As he begins elementary school, he is proud of the things he can achieve without his parents' help. His social circle widens, as friends (most, or all, of the same gender)

Family Challenge: Sibling Rivalry

In any family where there is more than one child, there's almost always some degree of sibling rivalry, as sisters and brothers compete with each other for their parents' attention. Sometimes, this can affect the siblings' eating habits. Consider this common family scenario: One child refuses to try new foods, while another eats almost anything. Some of that can certainly be due to genetic differences (perhaps Dad hates vegetables, while Mom loves them)—but chances are, sibling rivalry also plays a role.

After all, fussy eaters can drive their parents crazy, getting lots of attention even if it is negative ("why won't you even take a bite?"). That just sets the stage for another child to make a grab for attention, "winning" the eating game by cleaning his or her plate. This rivalry can become a routine, with the siblings assuming their roles of "picky eater" and "anything eater" and turning their eating habits into a competition.

What can a parent do? Stay on neutral ground, say experts. Don't make either sibling's eating an issue, either by heaping the "anything eater" with praise, or expressing frustration with the "picky eater." Instead, turn the table conversation to other subjects, and continue to model healthy eating habits yourself.

become a more important influence. Media (TV and computers) are starting to play a bigger role in his social life. He is better able to think logically, and, as he gets older, to better stay focused on a task from beginning to end. He can understand some basic principles of nutrition, such as categorizing foods (e.g., "breads and cereals" or "protein foods"), and the idea of balancing the food he eats ("energy in") with his activities ("energy out").

Parent Tip-offs—Food and Eating:

The Independent is ready for some responsibility.

- Include him in family meal planning, cooking and/or helping set the table or clean up.

- Continue to offer him a variety of foods, while modeling healthy eating habits yourself.

- Praise his growing skill with a knife and fork, as well as table manners.

- Introduce the idea of eating good foods to "fuel himself up" for his activities (and, of not overeating when he's not planning to be active later).

- Don't make it an issue if he suddenly shuns a former favorite food; chances are, he'll go back to liking it again someday. Food likes and dislikes can be highly influenced by peers.

- Let him have some say in planning his school lunch and after-school snacks. Provide a range of healthy foods choices that you know he likes, but the decisions should be his.

Parent Tip-offs—Activity:

- Look for activities you can all do together regularly, such as hiking or biking. As his physical skills grow, the Independent can participate more in family activity.

- Make it easy to pick up an activity: Keep the garage and/or playroom stocked with sports equipment.

- Introduce your child to organized sports, where he can learn how to be part of a team. Focus on having fun, not winning games.

- Focus on *your* positive skills ("I love riding my bike!") because he is absorbing his physical skills from his parents—so be careful not to label yourself negatively ("I'm not a good runner").

- Set reasonable limits on screen time now. Too much TV, computer or video games can prevent him from getting the "moving around time" he needs daily.

Age 11–13:
The Ever-changing Teen

Developmental Insights:

She can think more abstractly now, and can take time to reflect on what she learns. Her independent streak is stronger than ever, though she still needs occasional reassurance that you're keeping tabs on her. She's eating more meals away from home, and perhaps has spending money to make her own choices. She is now able to recognize the connection between eating behavior and good health, and is probably learning about nutrition at school. She's starting to look in the mirror a lot, and compare herself to others—no doubt she will find flaws, real or imagined. As she approaches puberty, her body begins to put on some fat; this may upset her. Organized sports at this age tend to become more competitive—and, for some children, more discouraging if they don't live up to "varsity" standards. Many girls at this age start to cut back on their physical activity; boys may begin to become less active as they approach their teen years.

Parent Tip-offs—Food and Eating:

- Ask for her input in planning "healthy" meals and snacks.

- Reinforce the idea of balancing the calories she takes in with the calories she burns in activity.

- Reassure her that this is a normal part of her growth process and will likely resolve with a growth spurt, if she's fearful of puberty fat.

- Be aware of what she's eating, without judging, and reassure her that "growing into her weight" is a safer, more effective option.

- Talk together about healthier options (say, getting plain pizza instead of pepperoni, or choosing a bag of nuts from a vending machine over a candy bar).

Family Challenge: Peer Pressure

As discussed earlier, children love to imitate their first role models: parents and caretakers. But as kids grow older, the opinions and behaviors of their peers become increasingly important. That can influence their ideas, and acceptance, of some types of foods. Your tween may no longer want to bring her lunch to school because her peer group considers it "uncool," for example, or she won't want to drink milk with her dinner because her best friend doesn't.

While this kind of behavior is perfectly natural, it can be frustratingly unpredictable for parents. But the best course, in most cases, is to stay neutral and work with your tween to find a solution you can both live with, rather than making food a focal point for arguments. Usually there is common ground that respects both parties: If she doesn't want milk with her dinner but you want her to get her daily milk servings, perhaps she can have a yogurt-based smoothie for an after-school snack instead. Or, if she wants to brown bag her lunch, put her in charge of making it—and give her a few ground rules to follow, such as "include at least one serving of a fruit and a vegetable." Stock the pantry with healthy foods for her to choose from (for ideas, see "The Healthy Family Pantry," pp. 36–38).

Of course, peer pressure can also work in your favor. If you're inviting one of your child's admired peers to dinner, find out about his or her favorite foods. If any are dishes you wish your child would try, go ahead and serve them. Knowing that her friend loves a dish might just compel her to try it!

Parent Tip-offs—Activity:

- Counteract the tween's tendencies to become less active, by continuing to make physical activity a priority.

- Inspire her to try other, less competitive sports options like karate, biking or hiking if she's no longer having fun in a team sport. As her body matures, she may even be ready for more "adult" exercise activities, such as yoga, aerobics and weight training.

- Encourage fun activities she and her friends can do together, such as in-line skating, skiing, tennis, snowboarding or swimming. Or, have her bring her friends along on family walks.

- Limit screen time—which now, likely, includes instant-messaging friends and video games.

Age 14–18: The Absorbed Adolescent

Developmental Insights:

As he readies himself for adulthood, he crosses many thresholds—puberty, high school, dating, a drivers' license—and, eventually, starting college or working life. He wants more freedom, but may need help understanding the responsibilities that come with it. He wants to distance himself from his parents, whom he won't miss a chance to challenge or criticize. At the same time, he is very sensitive when criticized himself.

His body is growing fast—with an appetite to match—but sometimes his physical development isn't as smooth as

Family Challenge: Rebellion

As a child grows into adulthood, he begins breaking away from home as he moves toward establishing his own identity. In the process, he's likely to challenge, or even shun, some of the values and beliefs he was raised with. During this "anything goes" period, he might experiment with dietary limits, too. Some teens try vegetarian diets of various forms, others, if competing in sports, might try special training-table diets to get in shape or perform better. And, if your teen is overweight, he might be experimenting with a weight loss diet.

Dieting in teens is a special concern, because their natural tendency to rebel—along with their typical belief that they are immune to danger—can sometimes lead them to make unsafe choices. One survey of over 8,300 teens found that one in four used unhealthy methods to lose weight, including smoking, skipping breakfast, taking laxatives or diet pills, and vomiting.

While you might have objections to the way your teen is eating, it's more important than ever not to criticize him. That can put him on the defensive, and he may dig in his heels even deeper. Your response to his behavior should stay consistent with your beliefs and values, but also respect that he has reasons for the choices he has made, too.

Instead of passing judgment, have a two-way conversation in which you both express your goals. Both of you might need to compromise to find some common ground. Of course, there's no common ground with unsafe behaviors like smoking or diet pills. Instead, suggest he consult with a registered dietitian, who can help him lose weight in a safe, effective way you're both comfortable with (see "Resources," page 244).

For your part, keep the expectations about family mealtimes consistent, and continue to make healthy foods available. You can accommodate his dietary needs within that framework — try offering a dinner entrée with the meat prepared separately, if he's a vegetarian. It's a great idea to encourage him to help with the family meal planning and preparation, too.

---

he'd like. He becomes increasingly self-conscious, and if he is overweight, he may have a low sense of self-esteem. He is probably not as he used to be, finding more sedentary ways to entertain himself. He may be interested only in exercise as a way of looking better (more muscular and/or leaner). While this may be great motivation to get him started, he'll be more likely to stick with regular exercise if he also finds it fun.

This is a time of pushing limits—including dietary ones. Many girls (and some boys) at this age experiment with weight loss diets—sometimes extreme, and eating disorders may be a concern. Expect the Absorbed Adolescent to try strange diets, live on fast-food, snack incessantly and more. Rapid bone growth means an increased need for calcium and iron—but like many teens, he might not be getting enough. His biological clock may switch to night-owl mode; he may skip breakfast because he's too sleepy. And, with a more active social schedule, he'll tend to miss more family meals.

Parent Tip-offs—Food and Eating:

- Make good-for-you foods available, so he can satisfy his hunger in a healthy way.

- Emphasize the concept of balancing the foods he eats with the amount of physical activity he gets.

- Keep the family beverage of choice milk (fat-free if possible) and provide other calcium-rich options, like yogurt, calcium-fortified orange juice, calcium-fortified cereals, canned salmon and dark leafy greens.

- Boost iron by regularly serving lean meats, iron-fortified cereals and breads, and other iron-rich foods.

- Provide him with easy, "grab and go" breakfast choices.

- Make sure he knows you still consider family mealtimes important, and that he is expected to attend (or to let you know in advance if he can't).

- Continue to provide healthy foods at home and model sensible eating behaviors yourself. Above all, avoid criticizing his eating choices.

- Seek professional advice immediately if you have concerns that your adolescent is developing an eating disorder—don't wait for the problem to go away on its own.

Parent Tip-offs—Activity:

- Fight back against the Adolescent's tendency to "sit more and move less," by continuing to make regular physical activity a focus of family life.

- Make it easy for him to pursue the activities he loves, but don't push him. If he is overweight, he may shun group sports.

- Cultivate a "one-on-one" shared sport with him, such as tennis, running or in-line skating. You'll cherish the bond later, as he separates from you in other ways.

- Limit screen time at home, including video games and instant messaging.

The Power of Activity

Virtually all of us are born loving to move our bodies; just watch any two-year-old for proof. But by the time we reach adulthood, many of us lose those healthy urges. At last count, one-quarter of Americans reported getting no exercise at all. And our children aren't faring much better: once they enter their teen years, their activity patterns tend to mirror those of adults. This lack of regular activity, experts believe, is one of the main reasons why obesity has become such a pervasive problem in this country.

That's where the power of the family team comes in. After all, since children learn lifelong habits from their families, it's never too late to start making regular activity one of those habits! Here's how to reclaim the joy of movement, and have fun along the way.

The Starting Line: Yourself

As with so much of parenting, being a good role model for your children can have a profound influence on their behavior. If you want your kids to become more active, then make sure you've gotten yourself off the couch first.

Even if you don't think of yourself as "an exercise person," you can find small ways to sneak a little more activity into your day. Use waiting time as get-fit time: jog in place as you wait for your computer to warm up, or stretch while you're waiting in line at the bank. Lift small weights when you watch

Stepping up Activity

For many people, walking is a great way to add more activity to their lives. After all, it's a skill at which most people past toddler-age are experts, and many people already do some walking as part of their days.

Experts suggest aiming for an additional 2,000 steps each day, which adds up to about one mile. While that sounds like a lot, it's easy to achieve if you think of adding steps in small amounts throughout the day. Try pacing back and forth every time you talk on the telephone, for example, or, if possible where you live, make it a habit to walk to local stores instead of driving. You can also put extra energy into everyday tasks like vacuuming to music or doing squats while pulling weeds rather than bending over. These extra steps will add up quickly, and over time, they'll lead to big changes!

One simple way to increase your steps is to wear a pedometer—a small device that keeps track of the steps you take daily, along with the distance traveled. Just wearing the pedometer can be motivating, because it gives you a visible way to assess your progress. For other creative ideas to increase your steps, check out "America on the Move," an organization that focuses on helping Americans find ways to eat less and move more (see page 247, for details).

TV, or do jumping jacks or sit-ups during commercials. Another good idea: practice a little fitness yourself when you drop off your kids at basketball or gymnastics practice, by walking or jogging around the facility where they are working out. Anything that gets you moving more qualifies, whether it's sweeping the floor, walking up an escalator instead of standing, or dancing to the radio.

A good goal to aim for is thirty to sixty minutes of this extra activity, most days of the week. If you have trouble squeezing in a thirty-minute block of time, try breaking it down into smaller amounts. A ten-minute walk after breakfast, lunch and dinner, for example, is an easy way to meet your daily goal. As you become more used to being active, you can gradually increase the amount of time, and the intensity, of your movements.

Mid-Game Strategy: Involve the Team

Once you've started making activity a bigger part of your life, you'll find it easier to bring the rest of family on board. Here are some ideas for turning a sedentary family into an actively moving team.

Schedule regular family activity. Most of us find it easier to make time for something if it occurs predictably, so why not make exercise a part of your family's regular routines? Tack activity onto something you're already doing together regularly—like taking a walk together after religious services.

More is better. The more activities you expose your children to, the more likely it is they'll find things that interest and challenge them. Explore your community for recreational facilities like walking clubs, sports teams or adventure outings. Or, try activities like walking local trails, bicycling or roller blading in-line skating. Good places to search are your local library or community center, community newspapers, local schools, organizations like the YMCA and area sports clubs.

Be the cheering section. If your child participates in organized sports, make it a point to attend games, preferably with the whole family along. Focus on having fun and being supportive, rather than dwelling on wins or losses.

Make your home sports-friendly. Keep the playroom stocked with balls, jump ropes, hula hoops and other activity equipment. That way your child will find it as easy to reach for them as for the television remote. Don't hesitate to use the equipment, too: you'll reinforce the message that activity is a family affair.

Turn off the set. Studies show that the more TV kids watch, the more likely they are to be overweight. After all, sitting in front of the tube keeps their bodies from getting the healthy movement they need. Set firm limits on how much TV your child can watch each day, and offer a positive alternative when you turn off the set—for example, "let's turn off the TV so that we can play hopscotch."

Involve the neighbors. Let your children invite neighborhood kids to your yard for games like Kick the Can, Capture the Flag, Flashlight Tag, Fox and Goose or croquet. They'll feel like leaders, while your family inspires others. Just about all kids love night games. All you need to do is let them run!

Have fun, and shake up the mix. Everyone's more likely to stick with an exercise routine if it's enjoyable, so make having fun a priority. Likewise, change or mix up the activity once in a while, so that no one gets bored or in a rut. Why not try a night at the roller rink instead of the usual family walk? Or wake up a family bike ride by renting a tandem bike or two?

Ask Dr. Hill:

Q. *"All of us in the family—kids and parents—are overweight. We have so much weight to lose it seems hopeless. Why bother?"*

A. Like any journey, weight loss begins with a first step—and that step is easier, and smaller, than you think. Small, gradual changes in eating habits and activity are easier to incorporate into the family's lifestyle than drastic ones, say experts, and they're more likely to "stick" for the long-term.

Focus on small, realistic goals—say, taking a ten-minute family walk after dinner three times a week. Or, depending on your kids' ages, run after them and play Hide 'n Seek, shoot a few hoops or hit a tennis ball back and forth. Achieving these goals can be powerfully motivating! Likewise, if the family has a lot of weight to lose, don't dwell on the number of pounds. Instead, define success in terms of health: for example, being able to climb the bedroom stairs for one minute without huffing and puffing. Make sure to celebrate each goal as the family reaches them, and continue to set new ones.

Don't be discouraged by those oft-cited statistics that suggest that many people who lose weight soon gain it back afterwards. That might lead you to believe there's no point in even trying. The truth is, a good many people succeed at both losing weight and keeping it off. Many document their success in the National Weight Control Registry—a catalog of over 5,000 successful "losers" who have lost at least thirty pounds, and kept the weight off for over a year. (Read more about the Registry in the "Resources" section on page 244.)

Q. *"I try to provide healthy food at home, but my kids are hardly ever around. I have little control over what they eat when they're at school, friends' houses or out in the community. What can I do?"*

A. The most important thing is something you're already doing: being committed to offering healthy foods, and modeling good eating behaviors, in your own home. That gives your children a valuable reference point for what smart eating looks like, no matter what environment they find themselves in.

But while good health begins with families like yours, it doesn't end there. The next step is to help create communities that support healthy eating and active living in general. There are many ways you and your family can get involved, depending on the needs of your community as well as your passions. Here, a few suggestions to get you started.

Support your local schools' recess, food service and nutrition education programs.

Advocate to improve the "walkability" of your community, with walking paths or sidewalks for walking and biking.

Coach, manage or donate time or funds to a neighborhood sports team.

Help create neighborhood "play days" or community-sponsored games.

Organize "pick-up" baseball, kickball or soccer games in your neighborhood.

Teach or support cooking classes for families and kids.

More ideas for supporting healthy communities can be found in the "Resources" section on page 244.

The Winner's Circle. Secrets of Successful Families

Today's families come in all shapes and sizes, but they share one common goal: preparing children for healthy, happy lives as adults. And, since home is the place children learn to establish lifelong habits, the family is "first base" in the weight loss game.

What does it take to win the game? While the strategies are many, they all work best when everyone acts together as a team. Each step family members take toward positive change—whether it's modeling good eating habits, making family dinners a priority or taking a nightly walk together—goes a long way toward making everyone healthier and strengthening family bonds. It all adds up to giving kids the skills they need for a lifetime of eating well and being active. And that's the best inheritance any family can pass on to its next generation.

The Healthy Family Pantry

Having a wide variety of the right ingredients on hand in your cupboard, refrigerator and freezer offers tremendous flexibility for preparing fresh, easy and great-tasting lower-calorie, lower-fat recipes. This pantry list covers the basics of good-for-you cooking, with room to add your families' favorites.

Fresh Produce:

Any fruit or vegetable in season

- Broccoli
- Cabbage
- Carrots
- Cucumbers
- Garlic
- Onions
- Potatoes
- Salad greens (any variety)
- Spinach and other leafy greens
- Sweet potatoes
- Apples
- Bananas
- Grapes
- Melons
- Oranges, tangerines and grapefruit

Dairy:

- Fat-free (skim) or low-fat (1%) milk
- Fat-free sour cream
- Plain fat-free yogurt
- Flavored fat-free yogurt
- Squeeze or tub margarine for spreading (also look for trans-free margarine)
- Light cream cheese
- Low-fat or reduced-fat cheese

Meats/Poultry/Fish:

Well-trimmed beef, pork and lamb cuts (e.g., "loin")

Skinless chicken and turkey

All types of shellfish and fish, especially fatty types (salmon, tuna); fatty fish is good—see page 147

Lean cold cuts (e.g., sliced roast turkey or beef)

Low-fat sausages (turkey)

Snacks:

Whole-grain crackers or flatbreads

Rice crackers

Whole wheat pretzels

Plain popcorn or low-fat microwave popcorn

Fig bars

Graham crackers

Cereals/Pastas:

Whole-grain cereals

Old-fashioned oatmeal

Whole-grain pasta

Quinoa, other grains

Canned and Bottled Goods:

Reduced-sodium broths

Reduced-sodium tomato soup

Canned beans

Canned no-salt-added tomatoes

Fat-free bean dip

Canned fruits (in water or fruit juice)

Oils and Dressings/Sauces:

Canola oil or soybean oil

Olive oil

Peanut butter

Low-fat or fat-free salad dressings

Sherry-, balsamic- and/or flavored vinegars

Pasta sauce

Salsa

Frozen Foods:

Soy burgers and crumbles (look for low-fat brands)

Frozen juices: cranberry, orange, apple

Low-fat frozen yogurt

Whole-fruit freezer pops

Bakery:

Whole-grain breads and rolls

Whole-grain English muffins

Whole-grain pitas

Corn tortillas

Whole wheat or white flour tortillas

Beverages:

Flavored sparkling water

100% fruit juices

About the Recipes

The recipes in this cookbook were selected and developed for time-pressed families—they are easy, convenient, kid-friendly, fun and use everyday ingredients.

The recipes were also chosen on the basis of health. Many contain fruits, vegetables, beans and whole grains. In most cases, they fall within reasonable levels for fat and sodium.

Canola, soybean and olive oils are called for throughout the book. They were chosen because they are heart-wise and health-wise fats to use for stir-frying, cooking and some baking. Because butter yields a tender product and gives great flavor to baked goods, you'll see butter used in the desserts chapter (although at a lower level than in many other cookbooks).

Skim milk is used whenever milk is called for, as that's an easy way to cut fat. Depending on the fat and calorie content of each dish, reduced-fat and fat-free dairy ingredients, like cream cheese and sour cream, may be called for. If a particular recipe is reasonable in fat content and calories, the regular product is used. If you usually use reduced-fat or fat-free, you may try them instead.

Because kids like eggs and they contain many nutrients, eggs are used, but you are given a choice of egg substitute or eggs, and the recipes work fine with either one.

Enjoy these recipes selected especially for families like yours.

Sunny Lemon-Raspberry Muffins (page 51) with
Key Lime–Banana Smoothie (page 67)

1

BEGIN WITH BREAKFAST

Nutty Whole-Grain Silver Dollar Pancakes

Prep Time: 25 Minutes   **Start to Finish:** 25 Minutes

6 servings (6 pancakes, 1 tablespoon yogurt and 2 1/2 tablespoons cereal mixture each)

note from
Dr. H:

Making sure you and your kids eat breakfast is a terrific way to start the day. Breakfast not only provides essential nutrients and valuable energy, but breakfast eaters tend to eat better overall than those who skip breakfast.

3/4 cup Wheaties® cereal, slightly crushed (1/2 cup)

1/4 cup raisins

1/4 cup dry-roasted sunflower nuts

2 cups Original Bisquick® mix

1 1/2 cups Wheaties cereal, crushed (3/4 cup)

1 1/4 cups fat-free (skim) milk

2 eggs or 1/2 cup fat-free egg product

1/3 cup vanilla fat-free yogurt

1. In small bowl, toss 1/2 cup slightly crushed cereal, the raisins and nuts; set aside.

2. Heat griddle or skillet over medium heat or to 375°F. Grease griddle with canola oil if necessary (or spray with cooking spray before heating).

3. In medium bowl, stir Bisquick mix, 3/4 cup crushed cereal, the milk and eggs with fork until blended. For each pancake, pour 1 measuring tablespoon batter onto hot griddle. Cook until edges are dry. Turn; cook other sides until golden.

4. For each serving, arrange 6 pancakes on plate. Top with 1 tablespoon yogurt and 2 1/2 tablespoons cereal mixture.

1 Serving: Calories 300 (Calories from Fat 90); Total Fat 10g (Saturated Fat 2.5g); Cholesterol 70mg; Sodium 750mg; Total Carbohydrate 45g (Dietary Fiber 2g; Sugars 13g); Protein 9g

% Daily Value: Vitamin A 8%; Vitamin C 2%; Calcium 20%; Iron 25%

Exchanges: 2 Starch, 1 Other Carbohydrate, 2 Fat

Carbohydrate Choices: 3

My kids and I wear step meters. We were shocked at how little exercise we were really getting.

Deb M.

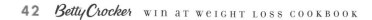

Whole Wheat Pancakes with Butter-Pecan Syrup

Prep Time: 25 Minutes   Start to Finish: 25 Minutes

8 servings (two 4-inch pancakes and 2 tablespoons syrup each)

BUTTER-PECAN SYRUP

2 tablespoons butter or margarine

1/3 cup chopped pecans

1/2 cup maple-flavored syrup

PANCAKES

1 1/4 cups all-purpose flour

3/4 cup whole wheat flour

1/4 cup sugar

2 teaspoons baking powder

1/2 teaspoon salt

1 1/3 cups fat-free (skim) milk

1/4 cup canola or soybean oil

1 egg, beaten, or 1/4 cup fat-free egg product

1. In 1-quart saucepan, melt butter over medium heat. Cook pecans in butter, stirring frequently, until browned. Stir in syrup; heat until hot. Remove from heat.

2. Heat griddle or 12-inch skillet over medium heat or to 375°F. Grease griddle with canola oil if necessary (or spray with cooking spray before heating).

3. In large bowl, mix flours, sugar, baking powder and salt. Stir in milk, oil and egg just until blended.

4. For each pancake, pour about 1/4 cup batter from cup or pitcher onto hot griddle. Cook 2 to 3 minutes or until bubbly on top and dry around edges. Turn and cook other sides 2 to 3 minutes longer or until bottoms are browned. Serve with syrup.

note from the nutritionist:

One serving of these yummy pancakes provides one of the whole-grain servings you need each day. A family goal to work toward is to eat three servings of whole grains daily. Easy ways to work it in? Try cereals, breads, waffles and pancakes.

1 Serving: Calories 330 (Calories from Fat 130); Total Fat 14g (Saturated Fat 2.5g); Cholesterol 35mg; Sodium 360mg; Total Carbohydrate 47g (Dietary Fiber 2g; Sugars 16g); Protein 6g

% Daily Value: Vitamin A 4%; Vitamin C 0%; Calcium 15%; Iron 10%

Exchanges: 2 Starch, 1 Other Carbohydrate, 2 1/2 Fat

Carbohydrate Choices: 3

Blueberry-Orange Pancakes with Blueberry-Orange Sauce

Prep Time: 35 Minutes   Start to Finish: 35 Minutes

7 servings (2 pancakes and about 3 tablespoons sauce each)

note from DR. H:

Positive self-talk is a powerful motivating tool. Rather than putting yourself down, think and talk positively about yourself to your kids. It can go a long way toward building your child's self-esteem (as well as your own!).

BLUEBERRY-ORANGE SAUCE

1/4 cup sugar

1 1/2 teaspoons cornstarch

2 tablespoons orange juice

1/4 teaspoon grated orange peel

2 cups fresh or frozen unsweetened blueberries

PANCAKES

2 cups Original Bisquick mix

1 cup fat-free (skim) milk

2 eggs or 1/2 cup fat-free egg product

1 teaspoon grated orange peel

1/4 teaspoon ground nutmeg

1 cup fresh or frozen unsweetened blueberries

1. In 1 1/2-quart saucepan, mix sugar and cornstarch. Stir in orange juice and 1/4 teaspoon orange peel until smooth. Stir in 2 cups blueberries. Heat to boiling over medium heat, stirring constantly. Boil about 2 minutes, stirring occasionally, until thickened. Keep warm while making pancakes.

2. Heat griddle or skillet over medium heat or to 375°F. Grease griddle with canola oil if necessary (or spray with cooking spray before heating).

3. In medium bowl, stir all pancake ingredients except blueberries with spoon until blended. Fold in 1 cup blueberries. For each pancake, pour slightly less than 1/4 cup batter onto hot griddle. Cook until edges are dry. Turn; cook other sides until golden. Serve with warm sauce.

1 Serving: Calories 230 (Calories from Fat 60); Total Fat 7g (Saturated Fat 1.5g); Cholesterol 60mg; Sodium 530mg; Total Carbohydrate 40g (Dietary Fiber 2g; Sugars 17g); Protein 6g

% Daily Value: Vitamin A 4%; Vitamin C 8%; Calcium 10%; Iron 8%

Exchanges: 1 1/2 Starch, 1/2 Fruit, 1/2 Other Carbohydrate, 1 Fat

Carbohydrate Choices: 2 1/2

Blueberry-Orange Pancakes with Blueberry-Orange Sauce

Cinnamon–Corn Bread Waffles with Apple-Cinnamon Syrup

Prep Time: 30 Minutes   **Start to Finish:** 30 Minutes

6 servings (two 4-inch waffles and 1/3 cup syrup each)

APPLE-CINNAMON SYRUP

1 cup cinnamon apple pie filling (from 21-oz can)

1 cup maple-flavored syrup

WAFFLES

1 1/2 cups Original Bisquick® mix

1/2 cup cornmeal

1 1/3 cups fat-free (skim) milk

2 tablespoons canola or soybean oil

1 teaspoon ground cinnamon

1 egg or 1/4 cup fat-free egg product

1. In medium microwavable bowl, mix pie filling and maple syrup. Microwave uncovered on High 2 to 3 minutes or until warm; set aside.

2. Heat waffle iron. (Waffle irons without a nonstick coating may need to be brushed with canola oil or sprayed with cooking spray before batter for each waffle is added.)

3. In medium bowl, stir all waffle ingredients with spoon until blended. Pour batter from cup or pitcher onto center of hot waffle iron. (Check manufacturer's directions for recommended amount of batter.) Close lid of waffle iron. Bake 4 to 5 minutes or until steaming stops. Carefully remove waffle. Repeat with remaining batter. Serve with syrup.

1 Serving: Calories 420 (Calories from Fat 90); Total Fat 10g (Saturated Fat 1.5g); Cholesterol 35mg; Sodium 530mg; Total Carbohydrate 77g (Dietary Fiber 1g; Sugars 30g); Protein 6g

% Daily Value: Vitamin A 4%; Vitamin C 0%; Calcium 15%; Iron 10%

Exchanges: 3 Starch, 2 Other Carbohydrate, 1 1/2 Fat

Carbohydrate Choices: 5

Cinnamon–Corn Bread Waffles with Apple-Cinnamon Syrup

Strawberry-Vanilla Yogurt Waffles

Prep Time: 25 Minutes   Start to Finish: 25 Minutes

6 servings (two 4-inch waffles, 1/4 cup sliced strawberries and 2 tablespoons syrup each)

1 1/2 cups all-purpose flour

3 tablespoons sugar

1 teaspoon baking powder

1/2 teaspoon baking soda

1/2 teaspoon salt

3 eggs or 3/4 cup fat-free egg product

1 container (6 oz) vanilla fat-free yogurt (2/3 cup)

3/4 cup fat-free (skim) milk or water

3 tablespoons butter or margarine, melted

1 1/2 cups sliced fresh strawberries

3/4 cup strawberry syrup, warmed

1. Heat waffle iron. (Waffle irons without a nonstick coating may need to be brushed with canola oil or sprayed with cooking spray before batter for each waffle is added.)

2. In large bowl, mix flour, sugar, baking powder, baking soda and salt; set aside. In medium bowl, beat eggs, yogurt and milk with wire whisk; beat in butter. Pour egg mixture all at once into flour mixture; stir until moistened.

3. Pour batter from cup or pitcher onto center of hot waffle iron. (Check manufacturer's directions for recommended amount of batter.) Close lid of waffle iron. Bake 4 to 5 minutes or until steaming stops. Carefully remove waffle. Repeat with remaining batter.

4. For each serving, arrange 2 waffles on plate. Top with 1/4 cup sliced strawberries and 2 tablespoons syrup.

note from Dr. H:

Focusing on what and how much you eat is important, but it's only part of the equation. The other big piece is how much you move. Become more active yourself, and encourage your kids to make moving a habit. You may all come up with a new discovery—that it's fun!

1 Serving: Calories 390 (Calories from Fat 80); Total Fat 9g (Saturated Fat 4g); Cholesterol 120mg; Sodium 530mg; Total Carbohydrate 71g (Dietary Fiber 2g; Sugars 31g); Protein 9g

% Daily Value: Vitamin A 8%; Vitamin C 20%; Calcium 15%; Iron 10%

Exchanges: 2 1/2 Starch, 2 Other Carbohydrate, 1 1/2 Fat

Carbohydrate Choices: 5

66 *Our late-night eating habits were getting to all of us. Now we try to eat well at each meal and not eat after 7:00 p.m.—well, most nights, anyway.* 99

Cheri O.

Crunchy Oven French Toast

Prep Time: 15 Minutes   Start to Finish: 35 Minutes

12 slices

2 tablespoons butter or margarine

5 tablespoons wheat germ

1/4 cup orange juice

2 tablespoons honey

3/4 cup fat-free egg product or
6 egg whites

12 slices French bread, 1 inch thick

1. Heat oven to 450°F. In 15x10x1-inch pan, melt butter in oven; spread evenly in pan. Sprinkle 3 tablespoons of the wheat germ evenly over butter.

2. In small bowl, beat orange juice, honey and egg product with hand beater until foamy. Soak each side of bread in egg mixture 2 minutes. Place in pan. Drizzle any remaining egg mixture over bread. Sprinkle remaining 2 tablespoons wheat germ evenly over bread.

3. Bake about 10 minutes or until bottoms are golden brown; turn. Bake 6 to 8 minutes longer or until bottoms are golden brown.

note from DR. H:

To become more aware of what you are eating and how much, learn to recognize what a healthy portion looks like. For a handy guide, see "Learn to Recognize Portion Sizes," page 17.

> *I've found that any recipe or food that I cook for myself at home is lower in fat and calories than anything I get at a restaurant as take-out or fast food.*
>
> Alyson S.

1 Slice: Calories 100 (Calories from Fat 25); Total Fat 3g (Saturated Fat 1g); Cholesterol 5mg; Sodium 150mg; Total Carbohydrate 14g (Dietary Fiber 0g; Sugars 4g); Protein 4g

% Daily Value: Vitamin A 4%; Vitamin C 0%; Calcium 2%; Iron 6%

Exchanges: 1 Starch, 1/2 Fat

Carbohydrate Choices: 1

Orange-Date Muffins

Prep Time: 15 Minutes   **Start to Finish:** 40 Minutes

12 muffins

1 1/2 cups whole wheat flour

3/4 cup all-purpose flour

3 teaspoons baking powder

1/2 teaspoon salt

1 cup fat-free (skim) milk

1/4 cup packed brown sugar

1/3 cup canola or soybean oil

2 teaspoons grated orange peel

1 egg or 1/4 cup fat-free egg product

1/2 cup chopped dates

1. Heat oven to 400°F. Grease bottoms only of 12 regular-size muffin cups with shortening (do not use paper baking cups).

2. In large bowl, mix flours, baking powder and salt; set aside. In medium bowl, beat milk, brown sugar, oil, orange peel and egg with fork or wire whisk until well mixed. Stir into flour mixture just until flour is moistened. Fold in dates. Divide evenly among muffin cups.

3. Bake 18 to 22 minutes or until toothpick inserted in center comes out clean and tops begin to brown. Run knife around sides of muffins to loosen. Remove from pan to wire rack. Serve warm.

note from the nutritionist:

At 3 grams per serving, these muffins are a good source of an often overlooked nutrient—fiber. Eating foods high in fiber gives you a sense of fullness that lasts throughout the morning.

1 Muffin: Calories 180 (Calories from Fat 60); Total Fat 7g (Saturated Fat 0.5g); Cholesterol 20mg; Sodium 240mg; Total Carbohydrate 28g (Dietary Fiber 3g; Sugars 11g); Protein 4g

% Daily Value: Vitamin A 0%; Vitamin C 0%; Calcium 10%; Iron 8%

Exchanges: 1 Starch, 1 Other Carbohydrate, 1 Fat

Carbohydrate Choices: 2

Sunny Lemon-Raspberry Muffins

Prep Time: 15 Minutes   Start to Finish: 35 Minutes

10 muffins

1 egg or 1/4 cup fat-free egg product

1 1/2 cups all-purpose flour

1 1/2 cups Whole Grain Total® cereal, slightly crushed (1 cup)

1/3 cup sugar

1/4 cup fat-free (skim) milk

1/4 cup canola or soybean oil

1 tablespoon grated lemon peel

2 teaspoons baking powder

1/2 teaspoon baking soda

1/2 teaspoon salt

1 container (6 oz) lemon fat-free yogurt (2/3 cup)

1/2 cup fresh or frozen (partially thawed) raspberries

1. Heat oven to 400°F. Line 10 regular-size muffin cups with paper baking cups.

2. In large bowl, beat egg slightly. Stir in remaining ingredients except raspberries just until moistened; gently stir in raspberries. Divide batter evenly among muffin cups.

3. Bake 15 to 20 minutes or until golden brown. Immediately remove from pan.

note from the nutritionist:

Adding cereal to baked goods is a great way to work in whole grains (check the cereal package to make sure it *is* whole grain). You also get the extra goodness of the vitamins and minerals, along with the great taste of lemon and raspberries, in these yummy muffins.

1 Muffin: Calories 190 (Calories from Fat 60); Total Fat 6g (Saturated Fat 0.5g); Cholesterol 20mg; Sodium 340mg; Total Carbohydrate 30g (Dietary Fiber 2g; Sugars 12g); Protein 4g

% Daily Value: Vitamin A 2%; Vitamin C 10%; Calcium 30%; Iron 25%

Exchanges: 1 Starch, 1 Other Carbohydrate, 1 Fat

Carbohydrate Choices: 2

Cranberry Corn Bread

Prep Time: 10 Minutes   **Start to Finish:** 40 Minutes

9 servings

1 1/4 cups all-purpose flour

3/4 cup cornmeal

1/3 cup sugar

2 teaspoons baking powder

1/2 teaspoon salt

2 eggs or 1/2 cup fat-free egg product

3/4 cup fat-free (skim) milk

1/4 cup canola or soybean oil

1 cup chopped fresh or frozen cranberries

2 tablespoons sugar

1. Heat oven to 400°F. Grease bottom and sides of 8-inch square pan with shortening or spray with cooking spray.

2. In large bowl, mix flour, cornmeal, 1/3 cup sugar, baking powder and salt. Add eggs, milk and oil; beat with spoon until mixed.

3. In small bowl, toss cranberries and 2 tablespoons sugar until coated. Fold into batter. Spread in pan.

4. Bake 25 to 30 minutes or until toothpick inserted in center comes out clean. Serve warm.

note from Dr. H:

Talk to your kids about the wholesome ingredients you use in baking and cooking. Involve them as much as possible in making dinner or breakfast on the weekend—chances are they'll be eager to help (and to eat what they've prepared!).

1 Serving: Calories 230 (Calories from Fat 70); Total Fat 8g (Saturated Fat 1g); Cholesterol 50mg; Sodium 260mg; Total Carbohydrate 35g (Dietary Fiber 2g; Sugars 12g); Protein 5g

% Daily Value: Vitamin A 2%; Vitamin C 0%; Calcium 10%; Iron 8%

Exchanges: 1 Starch, 1 1/2 Other Carbohydrate, 1 1/2 Fat

Carbohydrate Choices: 2

Blueberry Breakfast Cereal Bread

Prep Time: 30 Minutes   Start to Finish: 2 Hours 40 Minutes

1 loaf (16 slices)

2 cups Total® cereal, crushed (3/4 cup)

3/4 cup water

1 tablespoon grated orange or lemon peel

1/4 cup orange juice

1/2 teaspoon vanilla

2 cups all-purpose flour

1 cup sugar

1 1/2 teaspoons baking powder

1/2 teaspoon baking soda

1/2 teaspoon salt

2 tablespoons canola or soybean oil

1 egg or 1/4 cup fat-free egg product

1 cup fresh or frozen (thawed and drained) blueberries

1. Heat oven to 350°F. Grease bottom only of 9x5-inch loaf pan with shortening or spray bottom with cooking spray. In large bowl, mix cereal, water, orange peel, orange juice and vanilla; let stand 10 minutes. Stir in remaining ingredients except blueberries. Stir in blueberries. Pour into pan.

2. Bake 50 to 60 minutes or until toothpick inserted in center comes out clean. Cool 10 minutes. Loosen sides of loaf; remove from pan to wire rack. Cool completely before slicing, at least 1 hour.

note from Dr. H:

Try to make the dinner table a pleasant place to be, to encourage your kids to eat well. Keep the subjects light, turn off the TV and phone, and turn on the answering machine and the conversation.

1 Slice: Calories 150 (Calories from Fat 20); Total Fat 2.5g (Saturated Fat 0g); Cholesterol 15mg; Sodium 200mg; Total Carbohydrate 30g (Dietary Fiber 1g; Sugars 15g); Protein 3g

% Daily Value: Vitamin A 2%; Vitamin C 10%; Calcium 20%; Iron 20%

Exchanges: 1 Starch, 1 Other Carbohydrate, 1/2 Fat

Carbohydrate Choices: 2

Bacon, Cheese and Tomato Strata

Prep Time: 15 Minutes   Start to Finish: 3 Hours 15 Minutes

12 servings

7 cups lightly packed 1-inch cubes French bread (8 oz)

2 cups shredded reduced-fat Cheddar cheese (8 oz)

2 cups chopped plum (Roma) tomatoes (6 medium)

6 eggs or 1 1/2 cups fat-free egg product

1 1/2 cups fat-free (skim) milk

1 teaspoon Dijon mustard

1 teaspoon dried basil leaves

1/2 teaspoon salt

6 slices bacon

1. Spray 13x9-inch (3-quart) glass baking dish with cooking spray. Spread bread in baking dish. Sprinkle evenly with 1 1/2 cups of the cheese; mix lightly with bread. Sprinkle with tomatoes.

2. In medium bowl, beat eggs, milk, mustard, basil and salt with fork or wire whisk; pour over bread mixture. Cover tightly and refrigerate at least 2 hours but no longer than 24 hours.

3. Heat oven to 350°F. Bake uncovered 40 to 45 minutes or until knife inserted in center comes out clean. Meanwhile, in 10-inch skillet, cook bacon over medium heat 8 to 10 minutes, turning occasionally, until crisp; drain on paper towel.

4. Crumble bacon. Sprinkle bacon and remaining 1/2 cup cheese over strata. Let stand 10 minutes before serving.

1 Serving: Calories 160 (Calories from Fat 60); Total Fat 7g (Saturated Fat 2.5g); Cholesterol 115mg; Sodium 510mg; Total Carbohydrate 13g (Dietary Fiber 0g; Sugars 3g); Protein 12g

% Daily Value: Vitamin A 10%; Vitamin C 6%; Calcium 20%; Iron 6%

Exchanges: 1 Starch, 1 Medium-Fat Meat, 1/2 Fat

Carbohydrate Choices: 1

Bacon, Cheese and Tomato Strata

Chocolate Streusel Coffee Cake

Prep Time: 15 Minutes **Start to Finish:** 1 Hour 30 Minutes

9 servings

COFFEE CAKE

1 1/2 cups all-purpose flour

3/4 cup granulated sugar

1 teaspoon ground cinnamon

3/4 teaspoon baking powder

1/4 teaspoon baking soda

1/2 teaspoon salt

1/4 cup firm butter or margarine, cut into pieces

2/3 cup fat-free buttermilk

1 teaspoon vanilla

1 egg or 1/4 cup fat-free egg product

STREUSEL

1/4 cup all-purpose flour

1/4 cup packed brown sugar

1 tablespoon baking cocoa

1 tablespoon butter or margarine, softened

1/4 cup miniature semisweet chocolate chips

1. Heat oven to 350°F (if using dark or nonstick pan, heat oven to 325°F). Grease bottom only of 8-inch square pan with shortening or spray bottom with cooking spray.

2. In large bowl, stir 1 1/2 cups flour, the granulated sugar, cinnamon, baking powder, baking soda and salt until mixed. Cut in 1/4 cup butter, using pastry blender (or pulling 2 table knives through ingredients in opposite directions), until mixture is crumbly. Add buttermilk, vanilla and egg. Beat with electric mixer on medium speed 1 minute. Spread in pan.

3. In small bowl, mix all streusel ingredients except chocolate chips with fork until mixture is crumbly. Sprinkle over batter. Sprinkle with chocolate chips.

4. Bake 35 to 45 minutes or until toothpick inserted in center comes out clean. Cool 30 minutes. Serve warm.

1 Serving: Calories 280 (Calories from Fat 80); Total Fat 9g (Saturated Fat 4.5g); Cholesterol 40mg; Sodium 280mg; Total Carbohydrate 46g (Dietary Fiber 1g; Sugars 26g); Protein 4g

% Daily Value: Vitamin A 6%; Vitamin C 0%; Calcium 6%; Iron 10%

Exchanges: 1 1/2 Starch, 1 1/2 Other Carbohydrate, 1 1/2 Fat

Carbohydrate Choices: 3

Corn, Egg and Potato Bake

Prep Time: 20 Minutes **Start to Finish:** 1 Hour 30 Minutes

8 servings

4 cups frozen diced hash brown potatoes (from 2-lb bag), thawed

1/2 cup frozen whole-kernel corn (from 1-lb bag), thawed

1/4 cup chopped roasted red bell peppers (from 7-oz jar)

1 1/2 cups shredded reduced-fat Colby–Monterey Jack cheese (6 oz)

10 eggs or 2 1/2 cups fat-free egg product

1/2 cup fat-free small-curd cottage cheese

1/2 teaspoon dried oregano leaves

1/4 teaspoon garlic powder

4 medium green onions, chopped (1/4 cup)

1. Heat oven to 350°F. Spray 11x7-inch (2-quart) glass baking dish with cooking spray. In baking dish, layer potatoes, corn, bell peppers and 1 cup of the shredded cheese.

2. In medium bowl, beat eggs, cottage cheese, oregano and garlic powder with wire whisk until well blended. Slowly pour over potato mixture. Sprinkle with onions and remaining 1/2 cup cheese.

3. Cover and bake 30 minutes. Uncover and bake about 30 minutes longer or until knife inserted in center comes out clean. Let stand 5 to 10 minutes before cutting.

note from DR. H:

As your steps (or other physical activity) add up, so do the health benefits. Research shows that walking helps control blood pressure and cholesterol, while reducing the risk of diabetes, stroke and certain types of cancer.

1 Serving: Calories 260 (Calories from Fat 100); Total Fat 11g (Saturated Fat 4.5g); Cholesterol 275mg; Sodium 330mg; Total Carbohydrate 25g (Dietary Fiber 3g; Sugars 3g); Protein 17g

% Daily Value: Vitamin A 25%; Vitamin C 25%; Calcium 20%; Iron 8%

Exchanges: 1 1/2 Starch, 1 1/2 High-Fat Meat

Carbohydrate Choices: 1 1/2

Tex-Mex Turkey and Egg Bake

Prep Time: 20 Minutes   **Start to Finish:** 8 Hours 30 Minutes

10 servings

3/4 lb taco-seasoned ground turkey

5 cups frozen southern-style hash brown potatoes (from 32-oz bag)

1 can (4.5 oz) chopped green chiles, undrained

2 cups shredded reduced-fat Colby–Monterey Jack cheese (8 oz)

6 eggs or 1 1/2 cups fat-free egg product

1 1/2 cups fat-free (skim) milk

1 cup thick-and-chunky salsa

1. Spray 13x9-inch (3-quart) glass baking dish with cooking spray. In 10-inch skillet, cook turkey over medium heat 8 to 10 minutes, stirring occasionally, until no longer pink; drain.

2. Spread frozen potatoes in baking dish. Sprinkle with turkey, green chiles and 1 cup of the cheese. In medium bowl, beat eggs and milk with fork or wire whisk until well blended; pour over potato mixture. Sprinkle with remaining 1 cup cheese. Cover and refrigerate at least 8 hours but no longer than 12 hours.

3. Heat oven to 350°F. Bake uncovered 50 to 60 minutes or until knife inserted near center comes out clean. Let stand 10 minutes. Cut into squares. Serve with salsa.

note from DR. H:

Need more inspiration for physical activity? Find ways to build a more active environment where you live and work. Map out a walking route through your neighborhood or join co-workers in planning a walking route in or around your workplace.

1 Serving: Calories 260 (Calories from Fat 90); Total Fat 10g (Saturated Fat 4.5g); Cholesterol 160mg; Sodium 670mg; Total Carbohydrate 26g (Dietary Fiber 3g; Sugars 4g); Protein 19g

% Daily Value: Vitamin A 15%; Vitamin C 15%; Calcium 25%; Iron 8%

Exchanges: 1 1/2 Starch, 2 Lean Meat, 1/2 Fat

Carbohydrate Choices: 2

Get plenty of exercise and drink lots of water—that's a good way to stay healthy.

Clarke S. age 9

Breakfast Burritos

Prep Time: 25 Minutes   Start to Finish: 25 Minutes

4 servings

4 eggs or 1 cup fat-free egg product

2 tablespoons water

2 teaspoons butter or margarine

1/2 cup fat-free refried beans

1/4 cup thick-and-chunky salsa

2 flour tortillas (10 inch)

1/2 cup shredded reduced-fat Cheddar cheese (2 oz)

Reduced-fat sour cream, if desired

Chopped fresh cilantro, if desired

1. In small bowl, beat eggs and water with fork or wire whisk until well mixed.

2. In 10-inch nonstick skillet, melt butter over medium heat. Pour egg mixture into skillet. As mixture begins to set at bottom and side, gently lift cooked portions with spatula so that uncooked portion can flow to bottom. Cook 3 to 4 minutes or until eggs are thickened throughout but still moist; remove from heat and keep warm.

3. Spread refried beans and salsa on tortillas to within 1/2 inch of edge. Sprinkle with cheese. Place on microwavable plate; microwave each burrito uncovered on High 45 to 60 seconds or until tortilla and beans are very warm and cheese is starting to melt.

4. Cut eggs in half. Place each half on center of each tortilla. Fold top and bottom ends of each tortilla about 1 inch over filling; fold right and left sides over folded ends, overlapping. Cut each burrito in half. Serve with sour cream and cilantro.

note from the nutritionist:

Despite their name, refried beans don't have to be fried in oil or loaded with fat to be high in flavor. Look for the canned variety that is labeled fat-free. Refried beans are also a good source of fiber.

1 Serving: Calories 250 (Calories from Fat 100); Total Fat 11g (Saturated Fat 4g); Cholesterol 220mg; Sodium 560mg; Total Carbohydrate 25g (Dietary Fiber 3g; Sugars 2g); Protein 14g

% Daily Value: Vitamin A 10%; Vitamin C 2%; Calcium 20%; Iron 15%

Exchanges: 1 1/2 Starch, 1 1/2 Medium-Fat Meat, 1/2 Fat

Carbohydrate Choices: 1 1/2

English Muffin Breakfast Pizzas

Prep Time: 20 Minutes   **Start to Finish:** 20 Minutes

4 servings

1 cup fat-free egg product or 4 eggs

1/4 cup fat-free (skim) milk

Dash of salt

Dash of pepper

2 teaspoons canola or soybean oil

2 tablespoons chopped onion

2 tablespoons chopped red bell pepper

2 tablespoons chopped cooked ham

1/2 cup shredded reduced-fat Cheddar cheese (2 oz)

2 whole wheat English muffins, split, toasted

1. In small bowl, beat egg product, milk, salt and pepper with wire whisk or fork until well blended.

2. In 10-inch nonstick skillet, heat oil over medium heat. Cook onion, bell pepper and ham in oil 3 to 5 minutes, stirring occasionally, until vegetables are crisp-tender. Pour egg mixture into skillet. As eggs begin to set at bottom and side, gently lift cooked portions with spatula so that uncooked egg can flow to bottom. Cook 3 to 4 minutes or until eggs are thickened throughout but still moist; stir cheese into eggs.

3. Spoon egg mixture evenly over muffin halves.

1 Serving: Calories 150 (Calories from Fat 40); Total Fat 4.5g (Saturated Fat 1g); Cholesterol 5mg; Sodium 570mg; Total Carbohydrate 16g (Dietary Fiber 3g; Sugars 4g); Protein 14g

% Daily Value: Vitamin A 15%; Vitamin C 8%; Calcium 25%; Iron 10%

Exchanges: 1 Starch, 1 1/2 Very Lean Meat, 1/2 Fat

Carbohydrate Choices: 1

English Muffin Breakfast Pizzas

Plum Pudding Parfaits

Prep Time: 20 Minutes   Start to Finish: 20 Minutes

4 servings

1 package (4-serving size) vanilla fat-free sugar-free instant pudding and pie filling mix

1 1/4 cups fat-free (skim) milk

1 cup plain fat-free yogurt

1/2 cup low-fat granola

4 medium plums, pitted, chopped (about 2 cups)

1. Make pudding mix as directed on package—except use 1 1/4 cups fat-free (skim) milk. Fold in yogurt.

2. Place about 1/4 cup pudding mixture in bottom of each of 4 parfait glasses. Layer each glass with 1 tablespoon of the granola and about 1/4 cup of the plums; repeat layers. Top with remaining pudding mixture. Refrigerate until ready to serve.

1 Serving: Calories 170 (Calories from Fat 15); Total Fat 1.5g (Saturated Fat 0g); Cholesterol 0mg; Sodium 410mg; Total Carbohydrate 34g (Dietary Fiber 3g; Sugars 18g); Protein 8g

% Daily Value: Vitamin A 10%; Vitamin C 15%; Calcium 25%; Iron 4%

Exchanges: 1 Fruit, 1/2 Other Carbohydrate, 1 Skim Milk

Carbohydrate Choices: 2

Cinnamon-Pear Oatmeal with Toasted Walnuts

Prep Time: 20 Minutes   Start to Finish: 20 Minutes

4 servings

1 can (15 oz) pear halves in juice

2 cups old-fashioned or quick-cooking oats

1/2 teaspoon ground cinnamon

1/4 teaspoon salt

1/3 cup chopped walnuts, toasted*

1/4 cup packed brown sugar

1 cup fat-free (skim) milk

*To toast nuts, bake uncovered in ungreased shallow pan in 350°F oven 6 to 10 minutes, stirring occasionally, until golden brown. Or cook in ungreased heavy skillet over medium-low heat 5 to 7 minutes, stirring frequently until browning begins, then stirring constantly until golden brown.

1. Drain pears, reserving juice in 4-cup measuring cup. Add enough water to juice to measure 3 1/2 cups liquid. Chop pears; set aside.

2. In 2-quart saucepan, heat juice mixture to boiling. Stir in oats, cinnamon and salt. Cook over medium heat about 5 minutes for old-fashioned oats (about 1 minute for quick-cooking oats), stirring occasionally. Gently stir in chopped pears.

3. Spoon oatmeal into serving bowls. Top with walnuts, brown sugar and milk.

note from Dr. H:

A new way to serve oatmeal! The cinnamon and pears give it extra goodness and flavor, while the nuts pack an extra nutrition punch (but you can skip the nuts if folks at your house don't like them).

> *Try to start with at least one meal a day being meatless or low in fat.*
>
> Greg S.

1 Serving: Calories 330 (Calories from Fat 80); Total Fat 9g (Saturated Fat 1g); Cholesterol 0mg; Sodium 190mg; Total Carbohydrate 57g (Dietary Fiber 7g; Sugars 26g); Protein 10g

% Daily Value: Vitamin A 2%; Vitamin C 0%; Calcium 15%; Iron 15%

Exchanges: 1 Starch, 2 1/2 Other Carbohydrate, 1 High-Fat Meat

Carbohydrate Choices: 3

On-the-Go Oatmeal Bars

Prep Time: 15 Minutes   **Start to Finish:** 45 Minutes

20 bars

1/4 cup sugar

1/4 cup butter or margarine

1/3 cup honey

1/2 teaspoon ground cinnamon

1 cup diced dried fruit and raisin mixture

1 1/2 cups Wheaties® cereal

1 cup old-fashioned or quick-cooking oats

1/2 cup sliced almonds

1. Grease bottom and sides of 9-inch square pan with butter. In 3-quart saucepan, heat sugar, butter, honey and cinnamon to boiling over medium heat, stirring constantly. Boil 1 minute, stirring constantly; remove from heat. Stir in dried fruit. Stir in remaining ingredients.

2. Press mixture in pan with back of wooden spoon. Cool completely, about 30 minutes. For bars, cut into 5 rows by 4 rows. Store loosely covered at room temperature.

note from the nutritionist:

These breakfast super-snacks contain both ready-to-eat cereal and oatmeal, two great whole grains that are terrific together. Pack a couple in your backpack, lunch box or briefcase for a morning energy boost.

1 Bar: Calories 100 (Calories from Fat 35); Total Fat 4g (Saturated Fat 1.5g); Cholesterol 5mg; Sodium 35mg; Total Carbohydrate 17g (Dietary Fiber 2g; Sugars 11g); Protein 2g

% Daily Value: Vitamin A 4%; Vitamin C 0%; Calcium 0%; Iron 6%

Exchanges: 1 Starch, 1/2 Fat

Carbohydrate Choices: 1

Minerals that Matter

Calcium Counts

You already know that calcium helps build strong bones and teeth. But did you know that it also helps your nerves, muscles and heart function properly? It's especially important for children, because they need it to grow and to store for later in life. Here's the problem—most adults and children do not get enough calcium. However, you can increase your calcium deliciously and easily—just use the chart below.

Exercise—especially weight-bearing exercise—helps with calcium storage and makes bones dense and less likely to fracture. Go ahead, pump up your calcium and your exercise!

Top sources of calcium-rich foods:

Fat-free yogurt

Fat-free (skim) milk

Calcium-fortified orange juice

Chocolate milk

Reduced-fat mozzarella and reduced-fat Cheddar cheese

Salmon (canned with bones)

Soy milk (calcium-fortified)

Tofu (calcium-fortified)

Ready-to-eat cereals

Frozen yogurt

Cottage cheese

Oranges

Broccoli

When cooking, use fat-free (skim) milk in place of water in oatmeal, puddings and baking mixes.

It is possible to get calcium from supplements, but they are not recommended for kids, and research shows that your body absorbs calcium more readily from foods.

Increase Iron

You already know that iron builds healthy muscles and blood, but did you know that it also helps transport oxygen from the lungs throughout the body? And it's necessary for overall growth and development and the production of energy and immune system support.

Growing children, adolescents and women have the greatest need for iron. As with calcium, many adults and children do not get enough iron. Good news: you don't need an iron will to add more to your diet—just check out the chart below.

Top sources of iron-rich foods:

Red meat, especially beef

Eggs

Shrimp

Tuna

Oysters

Ready-to-eat cereals

Green leafy vegetables

Dried fruits

Enriched breads

When cooking, add crushed cereal to meat loaf mixtures, muffin batters and other baked goods to increase calcium and iron.

Your body more readily absorbs iron if you eat foods rich in vitamin C with an iron-rich food, like orange sections with a scrambled egg or tomato slices with a beef burger.

Creamy Peachsicle Smoothie

Prep Time: 5 Minutes   **Start to Finish:** 5 Minutes

3 servings (1 cup each)

1 cup frozen sliced peaches

1 banana, thickly sliced

1/2 cup vanilla fat-free yogurt

1 1/2 cups orange juice

1 tablespoon honey

1. In blender, place all ingredients.

2. Cover and blend on high speed about 1 minute or until smooth and creamy.

1 Serving: Calories 240 (Calories from Fat 0); Total Fat 0g (Saturated Fat 0g); Cholesterol 0mg; Sodium 30mg; Total Carbohydrate 56g (Dietary Fiber 3g; Sugars 50g); Protein 4g

% Daily Value: Vitamin A 8%; Vitamin C 220%; Calcium 8%; Iron 4%

Exchanges: 1 Fruit, 2 1/2 Other Carbohydrate, 1/2 Skim Milk

Carbohydrate Choices: 4

I like smoothies because they are tasty, healthy and easy to make. My mom likes them because they give me calcium.

Elizabeth H. age 8

Key Lime–Banana Smoothie

Prep Time: 5 Minutes   Start to Finish: 5 Minutes

2 servings (1 cup each)

1 container (6 oz) 99% fat-free Key lime pie yogurt (2/3 cup)

1 ripe banana, sliced

1/2 cup fat-free (skim) milk

1 tablespoon lime juice

1/4 teaspoon dry lemon lime-flavored soft drink mix (from 0.13-oz package)

1 cup vanilla frozen yogurt

1. In blender, place all ingredients except frozen yogurt. Cover and blend on high speed until smooth.

2. Add frozen yogurt. Cover and blend until smooth.

note from DR. H:

To avoid the unhealthful cycle of yo-yo dieting, make conscious changes to your eating habits and activity levels instead of dieting. For starters, eat about 100 fewer calories a day and increase your walking to 2,000 more steps a day.

1 Serving: Calories 320 (Calories from Fat 30); Total Fat 3g (Saturated Fat 2g); Cholesterol 10mg; Sodium 150mg; Total Carbohydrate 62g (Dietary Fiber 2g; Sugars 48g); Protein 11g

% Daily Value: Vitamin A 6%; Vitamin C 15%; Calcium 40%; Iron 2%

Exchanges: 1 Fruit, 2 Other Carbohydrate, 1 1/2 Skim Milk

Carbohydrate Choices: 4

Strawberry-Banana Yogurt Parfaits (page 93)

SATISFYING SNACKS AND APPETIZERS

2

Sugar 'n Spice Snack

Prep Time: 10 Minutes   **Start to Finish:** 1 Hour 15 Minutes

14 servings (about 3/4 cup each)

2 cups Corn Chex® cereal

2 cups Rice Chex® cereal

2 cups Apple Cinnamon Cheerios® cereal

3 cups Bugles® original-flavor corn snacks

1 1/2 cups dry-roasted peanuts

2 egg whites

2 tablespoons orange juice or water

1 cup sugar

1 teaspoon ground cinnamon

1. Heat oven to 300°F. Grease 15x10x1-inch pan with shortening or spray with cooking spray.

2. In large bowl, mix cereals, corn snacks and peanuts; set aside. In small bowl, beat egg whites, orange juice, sugar and cinnamon with wire whisk or hand beater until foamy. Pour over cereal mixture, stirring until evenly coated. Spread in pan.

3. Bake 45 to 50 minutes, stirring every 15 minutes, until light brown and crisp. Cool completely, about 15 minutes. Store in airtight container.

note from the nutritionist:

This recipe gives you a lot of goodness from the whole grains. Nuts are a great source of protein and good fat, but you can also use pretzels if you prefer.

1 Serving: Calories 230 (Calories from Fat 90); Total Fat 10g (Saturated Fat 2.5g); Cholesterol 0mg; Sodium 290mg; Total Carbohydrate 32g (Dietary Fiber 2g; Sugars 18g); Protein 6g

% Daily Value: Vitamin A 4%; Vitamin C 4%; Calcium 6%; Iron 20%

Exchanges: 1/2 Starch, 1 1/2 Other Carbohydrate, 1/2 High-Fat Meat, 1 Fat

Carbohydrate Choices: 2

This is a yummy sweet cereal snack. We made it on the weekend, and I put some in a little bag to take in my backpack to school. It's better for me than some snacks I was taking.

Carlon O. age 14

Peanut Butter Snack Bars

Prep Time: 10 Minutes   Start to Finish: 1 Hour 10 Minutes

12 bars

2/3 cup light corn syrup or honey

1/3 cup sugar

1/4 cup creamy peanut butter

6 cups Total Corn Flakes® cereal

1/2 cup dry-roasted salted peanuts

1. Grease bottom and sides of 9-inch square pan with butter. In 3-quart saucepan, heat corn syrup and sugar just to boiling over medium heat, stirring constantly. Remove from heat; stir in peanut butter until smooth. Gently stir in cereal and peanuts until evenly coated.

2. Press mixture in pan with back of wooden spoon. Let stand about 1 hour or until set. For bars, cut into 4 rows by 3 rows. Store loosely covered at room temperature.

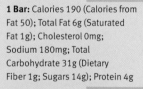

note from the nutritionist:

This bar makes a great snack or breakfast on the run! And it's loaded with iron, protein and calcium from the cereal and peanut butter. You can use any Total cereal in this easy recipe.

1 Bar: Calories 190 (Calories from Fat 50); Total Fat 6g (Saturated Fat 1g); Cholesterol 0mg; Sodium 180mg; Total Carbohydrate 31g (Dietary Fiber 1g; Sugars 14g); Protein 4g

% Daily Value: Vitamin A 4%; Vitamin C 20%; Calcium 40%; Iron 40%

Exchanges: 1 Starch, 1 Other Carbohydrate, 1 Fat

Carbohydrate Choices: 2

Seasoned Chicken Drummies

Prep Time: 35 Minutes   Start to Finish: 35 Minutes

20 to 24 servings (1 drummette and 1 tablespoon dip each)

1 container (16 oz) plain fat-free yogurt

1 tablespoon paprika

2 tablespoons curry powder

1 teaspoon garlic salt

20 to 24 chicken drummettes (about 2 lbs)

1/4 cup shredded peeled cucumber

1 clove garlic, finely chopped

1/2 teaspoon salt

1/2 teaspoon lemon juice

2 tablespoons chopped fresh mint leaves

1. In large bowl, mix 1/2 cup of the yogurt, the paprika, curry powder and garlic salt. Add chicken, stirring to coat all surfaces. Let stand 15 minutes.

2. Meanwhile, in small bowl, mix remaining yogurt and remaining ingredients. Sprinkle with additional chopped fresh mint leaves if desired.

3. Set oven control to broil. Place chicken on rack in broiler pan. Broil with tops 4 to 6 inches from heat 8 to 12 minutes, turning once or twice, until juice of chicken is no longer pink when centers of thickest pieces are cut. Serve with yogurt-mint dip.

To Grill: Heat coals or gas grill for direct heat. Prepare chicken and sauce as directed in steps 1 and 2. Cover and grill chicken over medium heat 8 to 12 minutes, turning once or twice, until juice of chicken is no longer pink when centers of thickest pieces are cut. Serve with yogurt-mint dip.

1 Serving: Calories 60 (Calories from Fat 20); Total Fat 2.5g (Saturated Fat 1g); Cholesterol 20mg; Sodium 140mg; Total Carbohydrate 3g (Dietary Fiber 0g; Sugars 1g); Protein 8g

% Daily Value: Vitamin A 6%; Vitamin C 0%; Calcium 6%; Iron 4%

Exchanges: 1 Lean Meat

Carbohydrate Choices: 0

Mini Barbecue Pizza Wedges

Prep Time: 10 Minutes   Start to Finish: 20 Minutes

12 servings

1 package (10 oz) prebaked personal-size Italian pizza crusts (2 crusts)

1/4 cup barbecue sauce

1/2 cup chopped cooked chicken

1 tablespoon chopped red onion

1 cup finely shredded part-skim mozzarella cheese (4 oz)

6 grape or cherry tomatoes, thinly sliced (1/3 cup)

1. Heat oven to 450°F. Top pizza crusts with remaining ingredients in order given. Place on cookie sheet.

2. Bake about 6 minutes or until cheese is melted and pizzas are hot. Cut each into 6 wedges.

To Grill: If using charcoal grill, arrange coals around edge of firebox. Heat coals or gas grill for indirect heat. Top pizza crusts with remaining ingredients in order given. Place pizzas over center of charcoal grill or over unheated side of gas grill. Cover and grill over medium heat 8 to 10 minutes, rotating pizzas occasionally, until cheese is melted and pizzas are hot.

1 Serving: Calories 110 (Calories from Fat 35); Total Fat 4g (Saturated Fat 2g); Cholesterol 15mg; Sodium 230mg; Total Carbohydrate 13g (Dietary Fiber 0g; Sugars 2g); Protein 7g

% Daily Value: Vitamin A 2%; Vitamin C 0%; Calcium 8%; Iron 4%

Exchanges: 1 Starch, 1/2 Medium-Fat Meat

Carbohydrate Choices: 1

Chicken Salad Roll-Ups

Prep Time: **35 Minutes**   Start to Finish: **1 Hour 35 Minutes**

24 servings

2 cups chopped cooked chicken

3 medium green onions, chopped (3 tablespoons)

1/4 cup chopped walnuts

1/2 cup creamy poppy seed dressing

1/2 cup reduced-fat cream cheese spread (from 8-oz container)

2 flour tortillas (10 inch)

6 leaves Bibb lettuce

1/2 cup finely chopped strawberries

1. In food processor bowl, mix chicken, onions and walnuts. Cover and process by using quick on-and-off motions until finely chopped. Add 1/3 cup of the poppy seed dressing; process only until mixed. In small bowl, mix remaining dressing and the cream cheese spread with spoon until smooth.

2. Spread cream cheese mixture evenly over entire surface of tortillas. Remove white rib from lettuce leaves. Press lettuce into cream cheese, tearing to fit and leaving top 2 inches of tortillas uncovered. Spread chicken mixture over lettuce. Sprinkle strawberries over chicken.

3. Firmly roll up tortillas, beginning at bottom. Wrap each roll in plastic wrap. Refrigerate at least 1 hour. Trim ends of each roll. Cut rolls into 1/2- to 3/4-inch slices.

note from Dr. H:

Planning ahead and keeping healthy snacks on hand is one way to tackle the between-meal hungries. Keep fresh fruits, veggies, yogurt, cereal, cereal bars, popcorn and granola bars in your refrigerator or cupboard.

1 Serving: Calories 80 (Calories from Fat 45); Total Fat 5g (Saturated Fat 1g); Cholesterol 15mg; Sodium 115mg; Total Carbohydrate 6g (Dietary Fiber 0g; Sugars 2g); Protein 4g

% Daily Value: Vitamin A 2%; Vitamin C 4%; Calcium 0%; Iron 2%

Exchanges: 1/2 Other Carbohydrate, 1/2 Lean Meat, 1/2 Fat

Carbohydrate Choices: 1/2

The step meters have really opened our eyes to how inactive we were. Now on the days when the number of steps is low, we go out and run around, throw a ball and try to keep our steps around 10,000 for the day.

Deb M.

Ham and String Cheese Bites

Prep Time: 25 Minutes   Start to Finish: 2 Hours 25 Minutes

25 servings

1 package (2.5 oz) thinly sliced ham

3 tablespoons garden vegetable reduced-fat cream cheese spread (from 8-oz container)

1 package (2/3 oz) fresh basil leaves

1/3 cup roasted red bell peppers (from 7-oz jar), patted dry

5 pieces (5 1/2 inches long) string cheese

1. Stack 2 slices ham on work surface; pat dry with paper towel. Spread evenly with 1 1/2 to 2 teaspoons cream cheese. Top with basil leaves to within 1 inch of top edge. Cut bell pepper into 1-inch strips; cut to fit width of ham. Place strip across bottom edge of ham. Place cheese piece above pepper on basil leaves; trim to fit.

2. Beginning at bottom, roll up securely. Wrap in plastic wrap. Repeat with remaining ingredients to make 5 rolls. Refrigerate 2 hours.

3. Unwrap rolls; place seam sides down. Cut each roll into 5 pieces with sharp serrated knife. If desired, pierce each roll with 5 evenly spaced toothpicks before cutting.

note from the nutritionist:

You can use regular cream cheese spread instead of the garden vegetable flavor. Just make sure it is the reduced-fat variety, which—besides being better for you—is softer and spreads more easily than regular cream cheese.

1 Serving: Calories 25 (Calories from Fat 15); Total Fat 1.5g (Saturated Fat 1g); Cholesterol 5mg; Sodium 75mg; Total Carbohydrate 0g (Dietary Fiber 0g; Sugars 0g); Protein 2g

% Daily Value: Vitamin A 4%; Vitamin C 8%; Calcium 4%; Iron 0%

Exchanges: Free

Carbohydrate Choices: 0

Cheesy Italian Tomato Toasts

Prep Time: 15 Minutes   Start to Finish: 35 Minutes

4 servings (2 pieces each)

note from the nutritionist:

Use good fats like canola or olive oil, like we have here. You may not notice the difference in taste, but your health will notice the difference— polyunsaturated and monounsaturated fats are better for your heart.

4 slices whole wheat bread, cut diagonally in half

1 large tomato, coarsely chopped (1 cup)

2 tablespoons chopped onion

2 teaspoons olive or canola oil

2 tablespoons chopped fresh parsley, if desired

1/2 teaspoon dried oregano leaves

1/2 teaspoon dried basil leaves

1/4 teaspoon garlic salt

1/4 cup shredded part-skim mozzarella cheese (1 oz)

1. Heat oven to 400°F. Place bread on ungreased cookie sheet. Bake about 5 minutes or until lightly toasted.

2. In small bowl, mix remaining ingredients except cheese. Top toast with tomato mixture. Sprinkle with cheese.

3. Bake 8 to 10 minutes or until bottom of bread is browned. Cool 5 minutes before serving.

1 Serving: Calories 120 (Calories from Fat 45); Total Fat 5g (Saturated Fat 1.5g); Cholesterol 0mg; Sodium 250mg; Total Carbohydrate 16g (Dietary Fiber 3g; Sugars 4g); Protein 5g

% Daily Value: Vitamin A 8%; Vitamin C 8%; Calcium 8%; Iron 8%

Exchanges: 1 Starch, 1 Fat

Carbohydrate Choices: 1

Cheesy Italian Tomato Toasts

Nachos in a Bag

Prep Time: 20 Minutes   Start to Finish: 20 Minutes

4 servings

1 can (15 to 16 oz) pinto beans, rinsed, drained

2 teaspoons reduced-sodium taco seasoning mix (from 1.25-oz package)

1/4 cup thick-and-chunky salsa

4 cups (4 oz) bite-size tortilla chips (about 80 chips)

1/2 cup shredded reduced-fat Cheddar cheese (2 oz)

1 small tomato, chopped (1/2 cup)

1/4 cup fat-free sour cream

4 medium green onions, sliced (1/4 cup)

1. In 1-quart saucepan, mix beans, taco seasoning mix and salsa. Heat over medium heat 6 to 8 minutes, stirring occasionally, until bubbly.

2. Place 1 cup of the chips in each of four 1-quart plastic food-storage bags. Squeeze bag to crush chips slightly.

3. Top chips with bean mixture. Divide remaining ingredients evenly among bags.

1 Serving: Calories 310 (Calories from Fat 80); Total Fat 9g (Saturated Fat 1.5g); Cholesterol 0mg; Sodium 640mg; Total Carbohydrate 50g (Dietary Fiber 10g; Sugars 4g); Protein 15g

% Daily Value: Vitamin A 10%; Vitamin C 8%; Calcium 20%; Iron 25%

Exchanges: 3 1/2 Starch, 1/2 High-Fat Meat, 1/2 Fat

Carbohydrate Choices: 2 1/2

Creamy Apple-Cinnamon Quesadilla

Prep Time: 20 Minutes   Start to Finish: 20 Minutes

4 servings (2 wedges each)

1/4 cup reduced-fat cream cheese spread (from 8-oz container)

1 tablespoon packed brown sugar

1/4 teaspoon ground cinnamon

2 whole wheat tortillas (8 inch)

1/2 small apple, cut into 1/4-inch slices (1/2 cup)

1. In small bowl, mix cream cheese, brown sugar and cinnamon with spoon.

2. Spread cream cheese mixture over tortillas. Place apple slices on cream cheese mixture on 1 tortilla. Top with remaining tortilla, cheese side down.

3. Heat 10-inch nonstick skillet over medium heat. Cook quesadilla in skillet 2 to 3 minutes or until bottom is brown and crisp; turn quesadilla. Cook 2 to 3 minutes longer or until bottom is brown and crisp.

4. Remove from skillet to cutting board; let stand 2 to 3 minutes. Cut into 8 wedges.

note from the nutritionist:

The whole wheat tortillas are the stars in this kid-friendly snack, which is so easy to prepare, the kids can make it on their own. If your family is not used to whole wheat tortillas, ask them to try something new—they may just like it!

1 Serving: Calories 90 (Calories from Fat 25); Total Fat 2.5g (Saturated Fat 1.5g); Cholesterol 10mg; Sodium 170mg; Total Carbohydrate 15g (Dietary Fiber 2g; Sugars 6g); Protein 3g

% Daily Value: Vitamin A 4%; Vitamin C 0%; Calcium 2%; Iron 4%

Exchanges: 1/2 Starch, 1/2 Other Carbohydrate, 1/2 Fat

Carbohydrate Choices: 1

Three-Cheese and Bacon Spread

Prep Time: 15 Minutes   **Start to Finish:** 15 Minutes

8 servings (about 2 tablespoons spread and 4 crackers each)

note from DR. H:

Kids will love making and spreading this out-of-the-ordinary sweet-and-savory spread on crackers. To keep fat low, it's important to read labels to see what's in the crackers you buy. Look for reduced-fat and whole wheat or whole grain whenever you can.

1/3 cup shredded reduced-fat Cheddar cheese

4 oz fat-free cream cheese, softened

1 tablespoon grated Parmesan cheese

2 tablespoons fat-free (skim) milk

1/8 teaspoon paprika

Dash of pepper

2 tablespoons real bacon bits

2 tablespoons raisins

1 medium green onion, thinly sliced (1 tablespoon)

16 water crackers or melba toast rounds

1. In small bowl, beat Cheddar cheese, cream cheese, Parmesan cheese, milk, paprika and pepper with electric mixer on medium speed until smooth.

2. Stir in bacon bits, raisins and onion until well blended.

3. Serve spread on crackers.

1 Serving: Calories 90 (Calories from Fat 20); Total Fat 2.5g (Saturated Fat 1g); Cholesterol 0mg; Sodium 250mg; Total Carbohydrate 13g (Dietary Fiber 0g; Sugars 2g); Protein 6g

% Daily Value: Vitamin A 4%; Vitamin C 0%; Calcium 8%; Iron 4%

Exchanges: 1 Starch, 1/2 Lean Meat

Carbohydrate Choices: 1

Any favorite recipe can be made lower in fat by using low-fat cheese, milk, sour cream or lean meat and by reducing butter and oil.

Alyson S.

Three-Cheese and Bacon Spread

Parmesan-Sesame Breadsticks

Prep Time: 15 Minutes   **Start to Finish:** 30 Minutes

12 breadsticks

2 cups Original Bisquick® mix

1/2 cup cold water

1/4 cup shredded Parmesan cheese

2 tablespoons sesame seed

1 tablespoon butter or margarine, melted

1. Heat oven to 450°F. Lightly grease large cookie sheet with shortening or spray with cooking spray. In medium bowl, mix Bisquick mix, water, 2 tablespoons of the cheese and 1 tablespoon of the sesame seed with spoon until soft dough forms.

2. Place dough on surface sprinkled with Bisquick mix; roll to coat. Roll into 10x8-inch rectangle. Brush with butter. Sprinkle with remaining cheese and sesame seed; press in gently. Cut crosswise into 12 strips. Gently twist each strip. Place 1/2 inch apart on cookie sheet.

3. Bake 10 to 12 minutes until light golden brown. Serve warm.

note from Dr. H:

These soft, tasty breadsticks are terrific with Beef-Barley Soup (page 123). Eating soup often is another healthy habit to build: you can work in veggies and fill people without a lot of calories—not to mention all the key nutrients you'll be getting.

1 Breadstick: Calories 110 (Calories from Fat 45); Total Fat 5g (Saturated Fat 1.5g); Cholesterol 0mg; Sodium 330mg; Total Carbohydrate 12g (Dietary Fiber 0g; Sugars 2g); Protein 3g

% Daily Value: Vitamin A 0%; Vitamin C 0%; Calcium 6%; Iron 4%

Exchanges: 1 Starch, 1 Fat

Carbohydrate Choices: 1

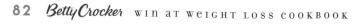

Fruit and Nut Bread with Browned Butter Glaze

Prep Time: 30 Minutes   Start to Finish: 2 Hours 55 Minutes

1 loaf (16 slices)

BREAD

2 cups Multi-Bran Chex® cereal, coarsely crushed

1 cup whole wheat flour

1 cup all-purpose flour

2 teaspoons baking powder

1/2 teaspoon salt

1 teaspoon pumpkin pie spice

1 egg or 1/4 cup fat-free egg product

1 1/3 cups fat-free (skim) milk

1/4 cup canola or soybean oil

1/3 cup dark molasses

1/2 cup chopped walnuts

3/4 cup diced dried fruit and raisin mixture

BROWNED BUTTER GLAZE

1 tablespoon butter
(do not use margarine)

1/2 cup powdered sugar

1 teaspoon vanilla

2 teaspoons water

1. Heat oven to 375°F. Spray 8x4-inch loaf pan with cooking spray; dust with flour. In large bowl, mix cereal, flours, baking powder, salt and pumpkin pie spice.

2. Stir in egg, milk, oil and molasses just until well combined. Stir in walnuts and dried fruit. Pour into pan.

3. Bake 45 to 55 minutes or until toothpick inserted in center comes out clean. Cool in pan 30 minutes. Remove from pan to wire rack. Cool completely, about 1 hour.

4. In 1-quart saucepan, heat butter over medium-low heat, stirring occasionally, until golden brown; remove from heat. Beat in remaining glaze ingredients with wire whisk until smooth; drizzle over loaf.

note from the nutritionist:

Don't tell the kids! This fabulous bread is really good for them. It has high fiber and many vitamins and minerals from the cereal and dried fruit. Because the overall fat and calories are low, you can enjoy the luscious glaze.

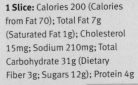

1 Slice: Calories 200 (Calories from Fat 70); Total Fat 7g (Saturated Fat 1g); Cholesterol 15mg; Sodium 210mg; Total Carbohydrate 31g (Dietary Fiber 3g; Sugars 12g); Protein 4g

% Daily Value: Vitamin A 4%; Vitamin C 0%; Calcium 15%; Iron 25%

Exchanges: 1 Starch, 1 Other Carbohydrate, 1 1/2 Fat

Carbohydrate Choices: 2

Carrot-Oatmeal Muffins

Prep Time: 15 Minutes   **Start to Finish:** 35 Minutes

12 muffins

1/2 cup old-fashioned or quick-cooking oats

1 cup fat-free buttermilk

1 egg, beaten, or 1/4 cup fat-free egg product

1/3 cup packed brown sugar

1/4 cup butter or margarine, melted

3/4 cup finely shredded carrot (about 1 medium)

1 1/2 cups all-purpose flour

1 teaspoon baking soda

1/2 teaspoon salt

1/4 teaspoon ground cinnamon

1 tablespoon old-fashioned or quick-cooking oats

1 tablespoon granulated sugar

1/4 teaspoon ground cinnamon

1. Heat oven to 400°F. Grease bottoms only of 12 regular-size muffin cups with shortening or spray bottoms with cooking spray.

2. In large bowl, mix 1/2 cup oats and the buttermilk with fork; let stand 5 minutes. Stir in egg, brown sugar, butter and carrot. Add flour, baking soda, salt and 1/4 teaspoon cinnamon; stir just until dry ingredients are moistened. Divide batter evenly among muffin cups (3/4 full).

3. In small bowl, mix 1 tablespoon oats, the granulated sugar and 1/4 teaspoon cinnamon. Sprinkle over batter in each cup.

4. Bake 15 to 20 minutes or until toothpick inserted in center comes out clean. Immediately remove from pan to wire rack. Serve warm.

1 Muffin: Calories 150 (Calories from Fat 45); Total Fat 5g (Saturated Fat 2.5g); Cholesterol 30mg; Sodium 260mg; Total Carbohydrate 23g (Dietary Fiber 1g; Sugars 8g); Protein 4g

% Daily Value: Vitamin A 30%; Vitamin C 0%; Calcium 4%; Iron 6%

Exchanges: 1 Starch, 1/2 Other Carbohydrate, 1 Fat

Carbohydrate Choices: 1 1/2

I hate carrots, love muffins, and when you put them together, I'll eat my carrots!

Elizabeth H. age 8

Carrot-Oatmeal Muffins

Fudgy Banana Pudding Pops

Prep Time: 20 Minutes   **Start to Finish:** 2 Hours 20 Minutes

8 servings

note from DR. H:

Between-meal snacks like these pudding pops are a great pick-me-up. They give you added energy and also help avoid the extreme hunger that can lead to overeating at meals.

1 package (4-serving size) chocolate fudge sugar-free fat-free instant pudding and pie filling mix

2 cups fat-free (skim) milk

1 medium ripe banana

1 container (6 oz) 99% fat-free vanilla yogurt (2/3 cup)

8 waxed paper cups (5-oz size)

8 wooden sticks with rounded ends

1. In medium bowl, beat pudding mix and milk with wire whisk about 2 minutes or until well blended. Let stand 5 minutes or until thickened.

2. Meanwhile, in small bowl, mash banana with fork. Stir in yogurt.

3. Place paper cups in 8-inch pan for easier handling. Spoon 2 tablespoons pudding into each cup. Divide yogurt mixture evenly among cups. Top with remaining pudding mixture. Tap cups on work surface to level top. Insert wooden stick into center of each pop.

4. Freeze pops about 2 hours or until solid. Store frozen pops in plastic freezer bag in freezer. Peel off paper cups before serving.

1 Serving: Calories 70 (Calories from Fat 0); Total Fat 0g (Saturated Fat 0g); Cholesterol 0mg; Sodium 190mg; Total Carbohydrate 14g (Dietary Fiber 0g; Sugars 8g); Protein 3g

% Daily Value: Vitamin A 2%; Vitamin C 4%; Calcium 10%; Iron 2%

Exchanges: 1/2 Other Carbohydrate, 1/2 Skim Milk

Carbohydrate Choices: 1

We still get to have little treats. If I want a treat for a snack or after dinner, I think back during the day—how many treats did I have? Can I have another small one?

Ruby O. age 9

Frozen Yogurt Crunch Cups

Prep Time: 20 Minutes   Start to Finish: 3 Hours 20 Minutes

12 servings

12 foil muffin cups

4 pouches (1.5 oz each) peanut butter crunchy granola bars (from 8.9-oz box)

1/4 cup chocolate-flavored syrup

4 cups vanilla fat-free frozen yogurt

1. Line 12 regular-size muffin cups with foil muffin cups. Leaving granola bars in pouches, crush granola bars with rolling pin.

2. Sprinkle crumbs from 2 pouches of granola bars evenly into bottoms of muffin cups. Drizzle 2 tablespoons of the chocolate syrup onto granola crumbs (about 1/2 teaspoon each). Spoon 1/3 cup frozen yogurt onto crumb mixture; smooth with back of spoon. Drizzle with remaining 2 tablespoons chocolate syrup. Top with remaining 2 pouches of granola crumbs. Press crumbs gently into top with fingers.

3. Freeze cups about 3 hours or until firm. Store tightly covered in freezer.

note from the nutritionist:

These yogurt cups have all the goodness of granola and the calcium of yogurt. More good news? The kids will love them and they are so easy to make. Look for snacks containing calcium and iron, as many kids don't get enough of these two important minerals.

1 Serving: Calories 150 (Calories from Fat 20); Total Fat 2g (Saturated Fat 0g); Cholesterol 0mg; Sodium 105mg; Total Carbohydrate 29g (Dietary Fiber 0g; Sugars 21g); Protein 4g

% Daily Value: Vitamin A 0%; Vitamin C 0%; Calcium 10%; Iron 4%

Exchanges: 1/2 Starch, 1 Other Carbohydrate, 1/2 Skim Milk

Carbohydrate Choices: 2

20 Smart Snacks with 150 or Fewer Calories

Snacking on low-calorie foods between meals actually does help keep energy and brain power at peak performance for both adults and children. . . . Smart snacking can also assure that your body's precious vitamin and mineral needs are met. Surprisingly, snacking can also help you control and maintain your weight because it helps prevent the extreme hunger that can lead to overeating.

An ideal snack contains a bit of protein and healthy fat for lasting energy, fiber to help keep you full and carbohydrates to give you an energy boost.

The snack chapter contains many tasty recipes, but you may not always have the time to cook something. In that case, use this handy list of snacks with 150 or fewer calories:

1. **Dry ready-to-eat cereals**—Whole-grain, fortified with vitamins and minerals (1/2 cup).

2. **Fresh fruits**—Bananas, frozen grapes, apples and kiwifruit are kid favorites (1 small or 1/2 cup).

3. **Vegetables**—Green bell pepper strips, baby-cut carrots, celery sticks, broccoli and cauliflower bites or any other veggies (1/2 cup).

4. **Low-fat yogurt**—High in calcium and protein, fat-free yogurt has even fewer calories (1/2 cup).

5. **Nuts**—Walnuts and almonds are rich in healthy fats and protein. And don't forget soy nuts (1 ounce).

6. **Dried fruits**—Raisins, dates, prunes and apricots contain much of the nutrition of fresh fruits (1/4 cup).

7. **Light popcorn**—Whole-grain, all-time family-favorite snack (3 cups).

8. **Whole-grain granola bars**—High in fiber and flavor; choose the lowest in sugar (1 bar).

9. **Low-fat cheeses**—Mozzarella or mozzarella string cheese is high in calcium and low in fat (1 string or 1 ounce).

10. **Soups**—Depending on the type selected, an 8-ounce serving is around 150 calories; look for low-sodium soups.

11. **Pudding**—High in calcium, choose low-fat (1/2 cup).

12. **Low-fat cottage cheese**—A great way to get calcium, fat-free has even fewer calories (1/2 cup).

13. **Frozen fruit bars**—Made from real fruit, these individual frozen novelties come in a rainbow of colors and flavors, like mango and strawberry-kiwi (1 bar).

14. **Sardines**—Even the ones packed in olive oil are around 120 calories; also high in calcium and iron (1 serving).

15. **Yogurt and fruit**—Combine 1/2 cup vanilla fat-free yogurt and half of a banana.

16. **Graham crackers**—Try with peanut or almond butter (4 crackers or 1 whole sheet and 1 teaspoon butter).

17. **Frozen grapes and reduced-fat Cheddar or mozzarella cheese**—Great combination (1 medium cluster grapes and 1 ounce cheese).

18. **Pretzels or chips**—Baked contain the fewest calories (1 ounce). Tortilla chips usually have fewer calories and less fat than potato chips.

19. **Animal cookies**—Sixteen little critters contain 120 calories.

20. **Whole wheat crackers**—Search for reduced- or low-fat to cut saturated and trans fats (1 ounce).

Cottage Cheese Dip with Cucumber Chips

Prep Time: 15 Minutes   Start to Finish: 15 Minutes

10 servings (about 2 tablespoons dip and 6 slices cucumber each)

2 cups low-fat cottage cheese

1/4 cup fat-free sour cream

3 tablespoons chopped fresh chives or green onions

1/2 teaspoon seasoned salt

1/4 teaspoon lemon-pepper seasoning

3 medium cucumbers, cut into 1/4-inch slices

1. In medium bowl, mix all ingredients except cucumbers.

2. Serve dip with cucumber slices.

note from DR. H:

When you want to make changes, it helps to set goals. Start small, and set ones that are doable for you, like "I will walk for 20 minutes after dinner three nights a week." When that goal has become a habit, set another goal.

My step counter counts my steps and I feel good when I reach my step goal.

North S. age 5

1 Serving: Calories 50 (Calories from Fat 10); Total Fat 1g (Saturated Fat 0.5g); Cholesterol 0mg; Sodium 270mg; Total Carbohydrate 4g (Dietary Fiber 0g; Sugars 3g); Protein 7g

% Daily Value: Vitamin A 4%; Vitamin C 4%; Calcium 4%; Iron 0%

Exchanges: 1/2 Other Carbohydrate, 1 Very Lean Meat

Carbohydrate Choices: 0

Dilly Beans

Prep Time: 20 Minutes   Start to Finish: 45 Minutes

4 servings

1 1/2 cups water

2 cups whole fresh green beans

2 tablespoons chopped fresh dill weed

1/4 cup thinly sliced onion

1/3 cup white wine vinegar

2 teaspoons canola or soybean oil

1/2 teaspoon sugar

2 cloves garlic, sliced

1/8 teaspoon crushed red pepper flakes

1. In 2-quart saucepan, heat water to boiling. Add beans. Cover and cook about 3 minutes or until bright green but still crisp; drain.

2. In medium bowl, toss beans, dill weed and onion.

3. In 1-quart saucepan, mix vinegar, oil, sugar, garlic and red pepper flakes. Heat to boiling; reduce heat. Simmer uncovered 2 minutes, stirring occasionally. Pour over green beans; mix well.

4. Cover and refrigerate 20 minutes or until serving.

1 Serving: Calories 45 (Calories from Fat 20); Total Fat 2.5g (Saturated Fat 0g); Cholesterol 0mg; Sodium 5mg; Total Carbohydrate 6g (Dietary Fiber 2g; Sugars 2g); Protein 0g

% Daily Value: Vitamin A 8%; Vitamin C 2%; Calcium 4%; Iron 2%

Exchanges: 1 Vegetable, 1/2 Fat

Carbohydrate Choices: 1/2

We eat a lot of vegetables at our house and I like them. Potatoes, baby carrots, cucumbers, corn, green peppers and green beans are my favorites.

Carlon O. age 14

Dilly Beans

Honey-Lime Watermelon Dunk

Prep Time: 15 Minutes   **Start to Finish:** 1 Hour 15 Minutes

4 servings

1/2 cup frozen (thawed) limeade concentrate (from 12-oz can)

1/3 cup water

1 tablespoon honey

4 cups 1-inch cubes watermelon

1. In small microwavable bowl, mix limeade concentrate, water and honey. Microwave uncovered on High 30 seconds. Stir until honey is dissolved. Refrigerate about 1 hour or until chilled.

2. To serve, spear watermelon chunks with toothpicks and dunk into limeade mixture.

note from Dr. H:

This is an incredibly fun snack for kids; they will love to watch the watermelon "soak up" the limeade mixture. And if eating is fun, kids will eat "healthy" without even noticing.

1 Serving: Calories 140 (Calories from Fat 5); Total Fat 0.5g (Saturated Fat 0g); Cholesterol 0mg; Sodium 0mg; Total Carbohydrate 33g (Dietary Fiber 0g; Sugars 29g); Protein 1g

% Daily Value: Vitamin A 15%; Vitamin C 30%; Calcium 0%; Iron 0%

Exchanges: 1 Fruit, 1 Other Carbohydrate

Carbohydrate Choices: 2

Our children are now eating a healthy diet, and we hope that continues in the future.

Greg S.

Strawberry-Banana Yogurt Parfaits

Prep Time: 15 Minutes **Start to Finish:** 15 Minutes

4 servings

18 reduced-fat vanilla wafer cookies, crumbled (about 1 cup)

2 containers (6 oz each) 99% fat-free strawberries and bananas yogurt (1 1/3 cups)

2 cups sliced fresh strawberries

4 whole strawberries, if desired

1. Reserve 2 teaspoons cookie crumbs for topping.

2. In each of 4 parfait glasses or dessert dishes, layer 2 tablespoons yogurt, 2 tablespoons cookie crumbs and 1/4 cup sliced strawberries. Repeat layers. Top with reserved cookie crumbs.

3. Garnish each parfait with whole strawberry.

note from the nutritionist:

This is a very easy, beautiful and tasty snack, with all the goodness of fruit. For even more nutrition, crush your favorite cereal and use it in place of the cookie crumbs.

Dad and I throw the baseball or football almost every day after school. Other kids come over and sometimes the whole neighborhood is in our yard playing baseball.

Christian O. age 17

1 Serving: Calories 190 (Calories from Fat 30); Total Fat 3g (Saturated Fat 1g); Cholesterol 0mg; Sodium 120mg; Total Carbohydrate 36g (Dietary Fiber 2g; Sugars 28g); Protein 5g

% Daily Value: Vitamin A 0%; Vitamin C 80%; Calcium 15%; Iron 4%

Exchanges: 2 Other Carbohydrate, 1/2 Skim Milk, 1/2 Fat

Carbohydrate Choices: 2 1/2

Bacon and Tomato Frittata (page 96)

3

Easy Dinners in 30 Minutes

Bacon and Tomato Frittata

Prep Time: 20 Minutes   Start to Finish: 20 Minutes

4 servings

1 carton (16 oz) fat-free egg product or 8 eggs

1/4 teaspoon salt-free garlic-and-herb seasoning

1/4 teaspoon salt

1 tablespoon canola or soybean oil

4 medium green onions, sliced (1/4 cup)

2 large plum (Roma) tomatoes, sliced

1/2 cup shredded sharp Cheddar cheese (2 oz)

2 tablespoons real bacon pieces (from 2.8-oz package)

2 tablespoons reduced-fat sour cream

1. In medium bowl, mix egg product, garlic-and-herb seasoning and salt; set aside.

2. In 10-inch nonstick ovenproof skillet, heat oil over medium heat. Add onions; cook and stir 1 minute. Reduce heat to medium-low. Pour in egg mixture. Cook 6 to 9 minutes, gently lifting edges of cooked portions with spatula so that uncooked egg mixture can flow to bottom of skillet, until set.

3. Set oven control to broil. Top frittata with tomatoes, cheese and bacon. Broil with top 4 inches from heat 1 to 2 minutes or until cheese is melted. Top each serving with sour cream.

1 Serving: Calories 180 (Calories from Fat 90); Total Fat 10g (Saturated Fat 4.5g); Cholesterol 20mg; Sodium 500mg; Total Carbohydrate 4g (Dietary Fiber 2g; Sugars 2g); Protein 17g

% Daily Value: Vitamin A 20%; Vitamin C 6%; Calcium 10%; Iron 15%

Exchanges: 2 1/2 Very Lean Meat, 2 Fat

Carbohydrate Choices: 0

My wife and I look forward to our evening walks. Besides getting much-needed exercise, this is the only time we get to talk without the kids.

Steve O.

Southwestern Potato Patties

Prep Time: 10 Minutes   Start to Finish: 25 Minutes

6 servings

1 bag (1 lb 4 oz) refrigerated Southwest-style shredded hash brown potatoes

3 eggs, beaten, or 3/4 cup fat-free egg product

1 cup shredded reduced-fat Cheddar cheese (4 oz)

1/2 cup Original Bisquick® mix

1/4 cup canola or olive oil

1 can (11 oz) whole-kernel corn with red and green peppers, drained

1 can (15 oz) black beans, rinsed, drained

1/4 cup thick-and-chunky salsa

1. In large bowl, mix potatoes, eggs, cheese and Bisquick mix.

2. In 12-inch skillet, heat 2 tablespoons of the oil over medium heat. For each patty, spoon about 1/2 cup potato mixture into oil in skillet. Flatten with the back of spatula.

3. Cook patties about 4 minutes, turning once, until golden brown. Remove from skillet and cover to keep warm while cooking remaining patties. Add remaining 2 tablespoons oil as needed to prevent sticking.

4. In 2-quart saucepan, heat corn, beans and salsa over medium heat 2 to 3 minutes, stirring occasionally, until hot. Serve over patties.

note from the nutritionist:

This recipe is a great dinner choice because it's easy, everyone will love it and, best of all, it's high in fiber. Fiber is important to maintain a healthy digestive tract and to help lower blood cholesterol levels.

1 Serving: Calories 420 (Calories from Fat 140); Total Fat 15g (Saturated Fat 3g); Cholesterol 110mg; Sodium 670mg; Total Carbohydrate 59g (Dietary Fiber 8g; Sugars 5g); Protein 17g

% Daily Value: Vitamin A 10%; Vitamin C 15%; Calcium 20%; Iron 15%

Exchanges: 4 Starch, 1 High-Fat Meat, 1 Fat

Carbohydrate Choices: 3 1/2

Chicken and Noodles Skillet

Prep Time: 10 Minutes   Start to Finish: 25 Minutes

4 servings

note from DR. H:

You'll notice that whenever fruits, vegetables or beans are added to a recipe, the vitamins and fiber really increase. That's because of all the important nutrients these foods provide. Adding them to recipes is an easy way to get your daily "dose" of these important foods.

1 tablespoon canola or soybean oil

1 lb boneless skinless chicken breast halves, cut into bite-size pieces

1 medium onion, chopped (1/2 cup)

1 cup baby-cut carrots, cut lengthwise in half

1 cup frozen broccoli cuts (from 1-lb bag)

1 cup uncooked egg noodles (2 oz)

1 can (14 oz) chicken broth

1 can (10 3/4 oz) condensed reduced-fat reduced-sodium cream of chicken soup

1. In 12-inch nonstick skillet, heat oil over medium-high heat. Cook chicken and onion in oil 6 to 8 minutes, stirring frequently, until browned and onion is just tender.

2. Stir in remaining ingredients. Heat to boiling; reduce heat. Cover and simmer 10 minutes. Uncover and simmer 5 to 8 minutes longer, stirring occasionally, until noodles are tender.

1 Serving: Calories 300 (Calories from Fat 90); Total Fat 10g (Saturated Fat 2g); Cholesterol 80mg; Sodium 800mg; Total Carbohydrate 23g (Dietary Fiber 3g; Sugars 3g); Protein 32g

% Daily Value: Vitamin A 120%; Vitamin C 20%; Calcium 6%; Iron 15%

Exchanges: 1 1/2 Starch, 4 Very Lean Meat, 1 Fat

Carbohydrate Choices: 1 1/2

> *I let each kid plan one dinner a week. They surprise me with the healthy choices they pick. Plus, with the ownership of planning the meal, they tend to eat better!*
>
> Deb M.

Lemon Chicken with Olives

Prep Time: 10 Minutes   Start to Finish: 20 Minutes

4 servings

4 boneless skinless chicken breast halves (about 1 1/4 lb)

1 tablespoon olive or canola oil

1 tablespoon lemon juice

1 teaspoon salt-free lemon-and-pepper seasoning

1/4 cup sliced ripe olives

4 thin slices lemon

1. Set oven control to broil. Spray broiler pan rack with cooking spray. Starting at thickest edge of each chicken breast, cut horizontally almost to opposite side. Open cut chicken breast so it's an even thickness.

2. In small bowl, mix oil and lemon juice. Drizzle over both sides of chicken breasts. Sprinkle both sides with lemon-and-pepper seasoning. Place on rack in broiler pan.

3. Broil with tops 4 inches from heat about 10 minutes, turning once and topping with olives and lemon slices during last 2 minutes of broiling, until chicken is no longer pink in center.

note from the nutritionist:

This wonderful lemon chicken is great served over long-grain rice. Try adding any green or orange vegetable (think green beans and carrots) or try a tasty vegetable salad. Want to know what's one serving of rice? It's one-half cup. To get used to what a serving looks like, use a measuring cup for a few meals.

1 Serving: Calories 210 (Calories from Fat 80); Total Fat 9g (Saturated Fat 2g); Cholesterol 85mg; Sodium 240mg; Total Carbohydrate 2g (Dietary Fiber 0g; Sugars 0g); Protein 31g

% Daily Value: Vitamin A 0%; Vitamin C 4%; Calcium 2%; Iron 8%

Exchanges: 4 1/2 Very Lean Meat, 1 1/2 Fat

Carbohydrate Choices: 0

Chicken Linguine Alfredo

Prep Time: 30 Minutes   **Start to Finish:** 30 Minutes

6 servings

8 oz uncooked linguine

2 teaspoons butter or margarine

2 tablespoons finely chopped shallot

1 clove garlic, finely chopped

1 pint (2 cups) fat-free half-and-half

3 tablespoons all-purpose flour

1/2 cup reduced-fat sour cream

1/4 cup shredded fresh Parmesan cheese

1/2 teaspoon salt

1/8 teaspoon white pepper

1 1/4 lb chicken breast strips for stir-fry

1 jar (7 oz) roasted red bell peppers, drained, thinly sliced

1/3 cup shredded fresh Parmesan cheese

2 tablespoons chopped fresh parsley

1. In 4-quart Dutch oven, cook linguine as directed on package. Drain; rinse with hot water. Return to Dutch oven to keep warm.

2. Meanwhile, in 2-quart saucepan, melt butter over medium heat. Add shallot and garlic; cook and stir 1 minute. In medium bowl, beat half-and-half and flour with wire whisk; add to saucepan. Heat to boiling, stirring frequently. Beat in sour cream with wire whisk. Reduce heat to low; cook 1 to 2 minutes or until heated. Remove from heat; stir in 1/4 cup cheese, the salt and pepper.

3. Heat 12-inch nonstick skillet over medium-high heat. Add chicken; cook about 5 minutes, stirring frequently, until no longer pink in center.

4. Add chicken, bell peppers and sauce to linguine; stir to mix. Cook over low heat until thoroughly heated. Garnish each serving with cheese and parsley.

1 Serving: Calories 410 (Calories from Fat 100); Total Fat 12g (Saturated Fat 6g); Cholesterol 75mg; Sodium 710mg; Total Carbohydrate 44g (Dietary Fiber 3g; Sugars 8g); Protein 33g

% Daily Value: Vitamin A 40%; Vitamin C 45%; Calcium 25%; Iron 15%

Exchanges: 3 Starch, 3 1/2 Very Lean Meat, 1 1/2 Fat

Carbohydrate Choices: 3

I like to jump rope for exercise—
I even made up a little poem:
'If you jump rope after dinner
You'll get a lot thinner.'
Elizabeth H. age 8

Chicken Linguine Alfredo

Chicken and Veggies Stir-Fry

Prep Time: 30 Minutes   Start to Finish: 30 Minutes

4 servings

note from the nutritionist:

Stir-frying is a healthy way to eat because it cooks meat and lots of vegetables with just a little oil. This lemony stir-fry is served over angel hair pasta, but you can also serve it over cooked Chinese noodles, vermicelli or rice.

8 oz uncooked angel hair (capellini) pasta

1 tablespoon canola or soybean oil

1 lb chicken breast tenders (not breaded), cut into 1-inch pieces

1 medium onion, cut into 8 wedges

2 cups small broccoli flowerets

1/2 cup sugar snap pea pods, strings removed

1 cup chicken broth

1 tablespoon chopped fresh or 1 teaspoon dried thyme leaves

1 teaspoon grated lemon peel

4 teaspoons cornstarch

1 1/2 teaspoons lemon pepper

1 cup cherry or grape tomatoes, cut in half

1. Cook and drain pasta as directed on package.

2. Meanwhile, in 12-inch skillet, heat oil over medium-high heat. Add chicken and onion; cook and stir 5 to 6 minutes or until chicken is brown.

3. Add broccoli and pea pods to chicken mixture. Cook over medium-high heat 4 to 5 minutes, stirring frequently, until vegetables are crisp-tender.

4. In small bowl, mix broth, thyme, lemon peel, cornstarch and lemon pepper; stir into chicken mixture. Cook over medium-high heat 1 to 2 minutes or until sauce is thickened and vegetables are coated.

5. Stir in tomatoes; cook until thoroughly heated. Serve over pasta.

1 Serving: Calories 430 (Calories from Fat 80); Total Fat 9g (Saturated Fat 1.5g); Cholesterol 70mg; Sodium 690mg; Total Carbohydrate 56g (Dietary Fiber 6g; Sugars 4g); Protein 36g

% Daily Value: Vitamin A 20%; Vitamin C 45%; Calcium 6%; Iron 25%

Exchanges: 3 1/2 Starch, 1 Vegetable, 3 1/2 Very Lean Meat, 1 Fat

Carbohydrate Choices: 3

Easy Ways to Fit in Fitness

Physical activity (as well as a healthy lifestyle) are important elements for successful weight loss and maintenance. Aim for at least 30 to 60 minutes of physical activity every day. If you can't fit in 30 minutes at a time, break it up by doing 10- or 15-minute "mini" workouts. Remember to check with your doctor before beginning any new workout, particularly if you are not used to exercising. Try these simple ways to fit in exercise:

Park farther away from your destination, whether it's at work, a restaurant or the mall.

Climb stairs and escalators (up and down) when possible.

Walk airport concourse corridors instead of standing on moving walkways.

Walk whenever you can: before work, during lunch, on breaks or after work.

Work out with a buddy to keep you motivated.

Try a new exercise or sport to break your routine. (How about yoga? Stretching and relaxing can be added benefits!)

Play with your kids: kick a soccer ball, dunk a basketball, toss a football, slam a volleyball, hit a baseball and run the bases, throw a Frisbee, jump rope, twist a hula hoop, ride a bike.

Walk your dog (or cat!). No pet? Borrow a friend's dog—they'll be delighted.

Use hand weights, an exercise ball, a rowing machine or a treadmill at home. Or pop in an exercise video and follow along.

Make more trips instead of fewer trips. Instead of carrying two bags of groceries into the house at the same time, take in one bag at a time.

Dust and clean your house, your office or your car—and have the kids help.

Dance around the house; get the kids and dance with them.

Be active when your kids are. Run after them or play with them at the playground.

Walk or bike during sports or other activities for your kids.

Play active childhood games like fox and geese, hide-and-seek, follow the leader, kickball and baseball.

Remember, any way that you can be more active counts. The point is to move more throughout the day.

Grilled Taco—Barbecue Chicken

Prep Time: 10 Minutes   Start to Finish: 10 Minutes

4 servings

note from the nutritionist:

For zesty, make-your-own wrap sandwiches, slice the warm chicken into strips and serve on whole wheat buns or in whole wheat tortillas with shredded lettuce, sliced avocado, chopped red onion and the special sauce.

2 tablespoons taco seasoning mix (from 1.25-oz package)

1 teaspoon dried oregano leaves

4 boneless skinless chicken breast halves (about 1 1/4 lb)

1 tablespoon olive or canola oil

1/2 cup barbecue sauce

1/4 cup chili sauce

1 teaspoon ground cumin

1. Heat closed medium-size contact grill for 5 minutes. In shallow bowl, mix taco seasoning mix and oregano. Brush chicken with oil; coat with taco seasoning mix. Place chicken on grill. Close grill. Grill 4 to 6 minutes or until juice of chicken is no longer pink when centers of thickest pieces are cut.

2. Meanwhile, in 1-quart saucepan, heat barbecue sauce, chili sauce and cumin to boiling over medium-low heat, stirring occasionally. Serve sauce with chicken.

1 Serving: Calories 270 (Calories from Fat 70); Total Fat 8g (Saturated Fat 2g); Cholesterol 85mg; Sodium 850mg; Total Carbohydrate 19g (Dietary Fiber 2g; Sugars 13g); Protein 32g

% Daily Value: Vitamin A 15%; Vitamin C 6%; Calcium 6%; Iron 10%

Exchanges: 1/2 Starch, 1/2 Other Carbohydrate, 4 1/2 Very Lean Meat, 1 Fat

Carbohydrate Choices: 1

Mandarin Chicken Salad

Prep Time: 10 Minutes   Start to Finish: 30 Minutes

5 servings

1/2 cup Original Bisquick® mix

2 tablespoons sesame seed

1 teaspoon ground ginger

2 tablespoons teriyaki sauce

1 tablespoon olive or canola oil

1 lb boneless skinless chicken breasts, cut into 1-inch pieces

1 bag (10 oz) European-style or romaine salad mix

1 can (11 oz) mandarin orange segments, drained

1 cup fresh snow (Chinese) pea pods, strings removed, cut in half if necessary

1/2 cup reduced-fat honey mustard dressing

1. Heat oven to 425°F. Spray cookie sheet with cooking spray. In 1-gallon resealable plastic food-storage bag, place Bisquick mix, sesame seed and ginger; mix well.

2. In small bowl, mix teriyaki sauce and oil. Coat chicken pieces with oil mixture. Shake about 6 chicken pieces at a time in bag of Bisquick mixture until coated. Shake off any extra mixture. On cookie sheet, place chicken pieces in single layer.

3. Bake 10 to 15 minutes or until chicken is no longer pink in center. Cool 5 minutes.

4. Meanwhile, in large bowl, mix salad mix, orange segments and pea pods. Top with warm chicken pieces and drizzle with dressing; toss to coat.

note from Dr. H:

Be a smart grocery shopper. Plan ahead what you will buy and make a list before you shop. Well-planned shopping may take more effort upfront, but you get a major payoff in knowing you will have the delicious and nutritious food you need for your family to create healthy meals.

1 Serving: Calories 290 (Calories from Fat 100); Total Fat 11g (Saturated Fat 2g); Cholesterol 55mg; Sodium 720mg; Total Carbohydrate 26g (Dietary Fiber 3g; Sugars 16g); Protein 24g

% Daily Value: Vitamin A 40%; Vitamin C 60%; Calcium 6%; Iron 15%

Exchanges: 1/2 Starch, 1 Other Carbohydrate, 3 Very Lean Meat, 2 Fat

Carbohydrate Choices: 2

Grilled Easy Steak Kabobs

Prep Time: 10 Minutes   Start to Finish: 30 Minutes

4 servings

note from the nutritionist:

Canola and olive are the oils called for in these recipes. Canola is the highest in polyunsaturated fat, and olive oil is high in monounsaturated fat, both good ways to eat wiser. You can convert any of your recipes that use vegetable oil to either canola or olive oil.

1 lb boneless beef top sirloin steak, cut into 24 one-inch pieces

1 medium bell pepper, cut into 16 one-inch wedges

16 medium mushrooms

1 tablespoon chopped fresh or 1 teaspoon dried dill weed

1 tablespoon lemon juice

1 tablespoon olive or canola oil

1 tablespoon honey mustard

1/4 teaspoon salt

1/4 teaspoon pepper

1. Heat coals or gas grill for direct heat.

2. On each of eight 10- to 12-inch metal skewers, thread beef, bell pepper and mushrooms alternately, leaving 1/4-inch space between each piece. In small bowl, mix remaining ingredients.

3. Cover and grill kabobs over medium heat 15 to 18 minutes, turning and brushing kabobs 3 or 4 times with oil mixture, until beef is desired doneness and vegetables are tender. Discard any remaining oil mixture.

1 Serving: Calories 180 (Calories from Fat 70); Total Fat 7g (Saturated Fat 1.5g); Cholesterol 60mg; Sodium 240mg; Total Carbohydrate 6g (Dietary Fiber 1g; Sugars 2g); Protein 25g

% Daily Value: Vitamin A 4%; Vitamin C 25%; Calcium 0%; Iron 15%

Exchanges: 3 1/2 Lean Meat

Carbohydrate Choices: 1/2

Skillet Beef, Veggies and Brown Rice

Prep Time: 30 Minutes   **Start to Finish:** 30 Minutes

4 servings

2 cups chicken broth

1 1/2 cups uncooked instant brown rice

2 medium carrots, sliced (1 cup)

2 teaspoons olive or canola oil

1/2 lb beef top round steak, cut into thin strips

1/4 cup chopped onion

1 cup sugar snap pea pods, strings removed

1 teaspoon Italian seasoning

1/4 teaspoon pepper

1. In 2-quart saucepan, heat broth to boiling. Stir in rice and carrots. Heat to boiling; reduce heat. Cover and simmer 6 to 8 minutes or until carrots are crisp-tender; remove from heat. Let stand 5 minutes.

2. Meanwhile, in 12-inch skillet, heat oil over medium-high heat. Cook beef and onion in oil about 8 minutes, stirring frequently, until beef is brown and onion is tender. Stir in cooked rice mixture, pea pods, Italian seasoning and pepper.

3. Cover and cook about 3 minutes, stirring occasionally, just until pea pods are tender. (Add a small amount of water to mixture if it becomes dry before pea pods are tender.)

note from DR. H:

Some people try to control their weight just by cutting back on calories. However, that's not the whole answer: Studies show that physical activity is critical to balancing energy and maintaining weight.

You walk on the treadmill and you work out with weights and you rest. That's exercise.

North S. age 5

1 Serving: Calories 280 (Calories from Fat 50); Total Fat 6g (Saturated Fat 1g); Cholesterol 30mg; Sodium 560mg; Total Carbohydrate 39g (Dietary Fiber 5g; Sugars 3g); Protein 18g

% Daily Value: Vitamin A 110%; Vitamin C 10%; Calcium 2%; Iron 15%

Exchanges: 2 1/2 Starch, 1 1/2 Lean Meat

Carbohydrate Choices: 2

Herbed Salisbury Mushroom Steaks

Prep Time: 20 Minutes   **Start to Finish:** 30 Minutes

5 servings

note from the nutritionist:

Using fat-free gravy and lean beef help you keep total fat and calories low. Round out this home-style meal with a side of steamed green beans and a simple mixed-greens salad.

1 package (8 oz) sliced fresh mushrooms (3 cups)

1 lb extra-lean (at least 90%) ground beef

1/4 cup plain dry bread crumbs

1 egg or 1/4 cup fat-free egg product

1/4 cup fat-free (skim) milk

3/4 teaspoon dried thyme leaves

3 tablespoons ketchup

2 teaspoons canola or soybean oil

1 jar (12 oz) fat-free beef gravy

1. Finely chop 1 cup of the mushrooms. In medium bowl, mix chopped mushrooms, beef, bread crumbs, egg, milk, thyme and 1 tablespoon of the ketchup. Shape mixture into 5 oval patties, 1/2-inch thick.

2. In 12-inch nonstick skillet, heat oil over medium-high heat. Cook patties in oil about 5 minutes, turning once, until browned.

3. Add remaining sliced mushrooms, 2 tablespoons ketchup and the gravy. Heat to boiling; reduce heat to low. Cover and cook 5 to 10 minutes or until meat thermometer inserted in center of patties reads 160°F and patties are no longer pink in center.

1 Serving: Calories 240 (Calories from Fat 100); Total Fat 11g (Saturated Fat 3.5g); Cholesterol 100mg; Sodium 590mg; Total Carbohydrate 12g (Dietary Fiber 0g; Sugars 4g); Protein 23g

% Daily Value: Vitamin A 6%; Vitamin C 2%; Calcium 4%; Iron 20%

Exchanges: 1 Starch, 3 Lean Meat

Carbohydrate Choices: 1.

Herbed Salisbury Mushroom Steaks

Peppered Pork in Mushroom Sauce

Prep Time: 30 Minutes   **Start to Finish:** 30 Minutes

4 servings

note from the nutritionist:

Baking, broiling, braising and roasting are the best low-fat ways to prepare meats because they add very little fat. Rosemary makes this dish taste special, but you can also try other herbs such as marjoram, thyme, parsley or oregano.

1 lb pork tenderloin

1 teaspoon mixed-pepper seasoning

1/4 teaspoon salt

2 teaspoons olive or canola oil

1 cup 33%-less-sodium chicken broth

2 tablespoons all-purpose flour

2 tablespoons balsamic vinegar

2 teaspoons dried rosemary leaves, crushed

1 package (8 oz) fresh whole mushrooms

1. Cut pork into four 4-oz pieces. Between sheets of plastic wrap or waxed paper, flatten pork pieces with meat mallet to 4x3 1/2 inches in diameter, less than 1/2-inch thick.

2. Sprinkle both sides of pork pieces with mixed-pepper seasoning and salt; press in seasonings. In 12-inch nonstick skillet, heat oil over medium-high heat. Add pork; cook about 5 minutes, turning once, until browned.

3. Meanwhile, in small bowl, mix broth and flour until smooth. Add broth mixture and remaining ingredients to skillet. Heat to boiling; reduce heat. Cover and cook 8 to 10 minutes, stirring occasionally, until pork is no longer pink in center and mushrooms are tender.

1 Serving: Calories 200 (Calories from Fat 60); Total Fat 7g (Saturated Fat 2g); Cholesterol 70mg; Sodium 420mg; Total Carbohydrate 7g (Dietary Fiber 1g; Sugars 1g); Protein 28g

% Daily Value: Vitamin A 0%; Vitamin C 0%; Calcium 2%; Iron 15%

Exchanges: 1 Vegetable, 3 1/2 Very Lean Meat, 1 Fat

Carbohydrate Choices: 1/2

Oven-Fried Pork Cutlets with Apple Slaw

Prep Time: 10 Minutes   Start to Finish: 30 Minutes

4 servings

PORK CUTLETS

4 boneless pork loin chops,
1/2 inch thick (about 1 lb)

8 saltine crackers, finely crushed
(1/3 cup)

1/2 cup Original Bisquick® mix

1/2 teaspoon paprika

1/4 teaspoon pepper

1 egg or 1/4 cup fat-free egg product

1 tablespoon water

Cooking spray

APPLE SLAW

4 cups coleslaw mix (shredded
cabbage and carrots)

1 small tart red apple, coarsely
chopped (1 cup)

1/4 cup chopped onion

1/3 cup fat-free coleslaw dressing

1/8 teaspoon celery seed

1. Heat oven to 425°F. Generously spray 15x10x1-inch pan with cooking spray. Between sheets of plastic wrap or waxed paper, flatten each pork chop with meat mallet to about 1/4-inch thickness.

2. In small shallow dish, mix crackers, Bisquick mix, paprika and pepper. In another shallow dish, beat egg and water. Dip pork chops into egg, then coat with Bisquick mixture. Repeat dipping coated pork in egg and in Bisquick mixture. Place in pan. Generously spray tops of pork with cooking spray.

3. Bake about 20 minutes or until pork chops are golden brown and no longer pink in center.

4. Meanwhile, in large bowl, toss all apple slaw ingredients. Place slaw on serving platter; arrange pork on top.

> *I like helping Mom in the kitchen. We make dinner together sometimes. It seems like the days I help, I feel more like eating.*
>
> Carlon O. age 14

note from DR. H:

Assigning jobs for meals to each family member makes them feel like part of the team. Setting the table, fixing a salad and clearing and washing the dishes are all tasks that they can help with.

1 Serving: Calories 350 (Calories from Fat 120); Total Fat 13g (Saturated Fat 4g); Cholesterol 125mg; Sodium 540mg; Total Carbohydrate 31g (Dietary Fiber 4g; Sugars 12g); Protein 29g

% Daily Value: Vitamin A 120%; Vitamin C 20%; Calcium 10%; Iron 15%

Exchanges: 1/2 Starch, 1 Other Carbohydrate, 1 Vegetable, 3 1/2 Lean Meat, 1/2 Fat

Carbohydrate Choices: 2

Cajun-Smothered Pork Chops

Prep Time: 15 Minutes **Start to Finish:** 15 Minutes

4 servings

4 bone-in pork loin chops, 1/2 inch thick (about 1 lb)

2 teaspoons salt-free extra-spicy seasoning blend

2 teaspoons canola or olive oil

1/2 medium onion, sliced

1 can (14.5 oz) zesty diced tomatoes with jalapeño peppers, undrained

1. Sprinkle both sides of pork chops with seasoning blend. In 12-inch nonstick skillet, heat oil over medium-high heat. Cook onion in oil about 2 minutes, stirring occasionally, until slightly tender. Move onion to one side of skillet.

2. Add pork to other side of skillet. Cook about 3 minutes, turning once, until browned. Add tomatoes. Heat to boiling; reduce heat. Cover and cook 4 to 8 minutes or until pork is no longer pink in center.

note from Dr. H:

You are the most important role model in your children's lives, so take care of yourself: eat healthy and stay active. You can turn these spicy pork chops into a meal by serving them with hot cooked rice or pasta.

1 Serving: Calories 230 (Calories from Fat 100); Total Fat 11g (Saturated Fat 3g); Cholesterol 70mg; Sodium 330mg; Total Carbohydrate 9g (Dietary Fiber 1g; Sugars 6g); Protein 25g

% Daily Value: Vitamin A 6%; Vitamin C 10%; Calcium 4%; Iron 8%

Exchanges: 1/2 Starch, 3 1/2 Lean Meat

Carbohydrate Choices: 1/2

Southwest Pork Soup

Prep Time: 20 Minutes   Start to Finish: 30 Minutes

5 servings (1 1/4 cups each)

2 teaspoons canola or soybean oil

1 lb boneless pork loin, cut into 1/2-inch cubes

4 medium green onions, sliced (1/4 cup)

1 small jalapeño chile, seeded, finely chopped

1 clove garlic, finely chopped

2 cans (14 oz each) 33%-less-sodium chicken broth

2 cans (15 to 16 oz each) great northern beans, rinsed, drained

1/2 cup loosely packed chopped fresh cilantro

1/4 cup loosely packed chopped fresh parsley

1. In 3-quart nonstick saucepan, heat oil over medium-high heat. Cook pork in oil 3 to 5 minutes, stirring occasionally, until brown. Add onions, chile and garlic; cook and stir 1 minute.

2. Stir in broth and beans. Heat to boiling; reduce heat. Cover and simmer about 10 minutes or until pork is no longer pink in center. Stir in cilantro and parsley; cook until heated through.

note from DR. H:

Research shows that filling up on watery foods (soups, fruits and vegetables) that contain fewer calories than denser foods, may help you maintain your weight, and you may even lose weight. This has been referred to as *volumetrics* or calorie density.

It was frustrating when my weight was more than my height, but I kept eating a lot of soup, watery fruits and vegetables and I'd ride my bike a lot. Now I finally grew a little and my height caught up with my weight. It feels good.

Carlon O. age 14

1 Serving: Calories 350 (Calories from Fat 80); Total Fat 9g (Saturated Fat 2.5g); Cholesterol 55mg; Sodium 410mg; Total Carbohydrate 39g (Dietary Fiber 10g; Sugars 1g); Protein 36g

% Daily Value: Vitamin A 8%; Vitamin C 6%; Calcium 15%; Iron 40%

Exchanges: 2 1/2 Starch, 4 Very Lean Meat, 1 Fat

Carbohydrate Choices: 2

Chicken-Vegetable Soup with Dumplings

Prep Time: 10 Minutes   **Start to Finish:** 30 Minutes

6 servings (1 cup each)

2 cups cut-up cooked chicken

4 cups 33%-less-sodium chicken broth (from three 14-oz cans)

1 tablespoon chopped fresh parsley

1 tablespoon chopped fresh thyme leaves

2 cloves garlic, finely chopped

1 bag (1 lb) frozen mixed vegetables, thawed, drained

1 cup Original Bisquick® mix

1/3 cup milk

1. In 3-quart saucepan, heat all ingredients except Bisquick mix and milk to boiling, stirring occasionally.

2. In small bowl, stir Bisquick mix and milk with fork until soft dough forms. Drop dough by 18 teaspoonfuls onto boiling soup. If dumplings sink into soup, carefully bring them to top of broth using slotted spoon. Reduce heat to medium-low.

3. Cook uncovered 10 minutes. Cover and cook 15 minutes longer.

note from the nutritionist:

Loaded with nutrients, this chicken soup is also outstanding in flavor. You can use any combination of frozen vegetables your family enjoys in this extra-easy recipe.

1 Serving: Calories 240 (Calories from Fat 80); Total Fat 9g (Saturated Fat 2.5g); Cholesterol 40mg; Sodium 720mg; Total Carbohydrate 23g (Dietary Fiber 4g; Sugars 5g); Protein 18g

% Daily Value: Vitamin A 70%; Vitamin C 4%; Calcium 10%; Iron 15%

Exchanges: 1 1/2 Starch, 1/2 Vegetable, 1 1/2 Lean Meat, 1 Fat

Carbohydrate Choices: 1 1/2

" I get a lot of help from my wife. She insists on a healthy dinner, so even when I mess up breakfast and lunch on my own, I get one reasonable meal each day. Now if I would only take those leftovers for lunch . . . that would make it two out of three. "

Greg S.

Chicken-Vegetable Soup with Dumplings

Chunky Tomato Soup

Prep Time: 10 Minutes **Start to Finish:** 30 Minutes

6 servings (2 cups each)

2 tablespoons olive or canola oil

2 cloves garlic, finely chopped

2 medium stalks celery, coarsely chopped (1 cup)

2 medium carrots, coarsely chopped (1 cup)

2 cans (28 oz each) Italian-style (plum) tomatoes, undrained

2 cups water

2 teaspoons dried basil leaves

1/2 teaspoon pepper

2 cans (14 oz each) chicken broth

1. In 5- or 6-quart Dutch oven, heat oil over medium-high heat. Cook garlic, celery and carrots in oil 5 to 7 minutes, stirring frequently, until carrots are crisp-tender.

2. Stir in tomatoes, breaking up tomatoes coarsely. Stir in water, basil, pepper and broth. Heat to boiling; reduce heat to low.

3. Cover and simmer 20 minutes, stirring occasionally.

note from the nutritionist:

Open-face mozzarella cheese toasts make a great partner for this veggie soup, along with tall glasses of ice-cold milk to increase the protein in this meatless meal. Toast the bread first, sprinkle a little shredded cheese over the top and microwave for 20 to 30 seconds to melt.

1 Serving: Calories 130 (Calories from Fat 50); Total Fat 6g (Saturated Fat 1g); Cholesterol 0mg; Sodium 980mg; Total Carbohydrate 16g (Dietary Fiber 4g; Sugars 7g); Protein 6g

% Daily Value: Vitamin A 100%; Vitamin C 35%; Calcium 10%; Iron 10%

Exchanges: 1/2 Starch, 1 1/2 Vegetable, 1 1/2 Fat

Carbohydrate Choices: 1

I like the cooked vegetables in soup. They just taste better than the fresh ones. And they're softer and easier to eat.

Ruby O. age 9

Bean and Cheese Skillet Supper

Prep Time: 25 Minutes **Start to Finish:** 25 Minutes

4 servings

1 cup frozen whole-kernel corn
(from 1-lb bag) or fresh corn kernels

2 tablespoons chopped fresh cilantro

1 small green bell pepper, chopped
(1/2 cup)

1 small onion, chopped (1/4 cup)

1 can (15 to 16 oz) kidney beans,
undrained

1 can (15 oz) black beans,
rinsed, drained

1 cup shredded Mexican Cheddar
Jack cheese blend with jalapeño
peppers (4 oz)

2 medium tomatoes,
chopped (1 1/2 cups)

1. In 12-inch skillet, mix all ingredients except cheese and tomatoes. Heat to boiling; reduce heat. Cover and simmer 5 minutes.

2. Uncover and simmer 5 to 10 minutes, stirring occasionally, until vegetables are tender. Stir in cheese and tomatoes until cheese is melted.

note from the nutritionist:

This recipe has a great nutrition story: high fiber from the beans; high in calcium from the cheese; high in vitamins A and C from the veggies.

> *We like this recipe because we are trying to eat less meat. When you combine the beans, veggies and cheese like this recipe does, my family doesn't even miss the meat.*
>
> Cheri O.

1 Serving: Calories 370 (Calories from Fat 80); Total Fat 8g (Saturated Fat 4.5g); Cholesterol 25mg; Sodium 790mg; Total Carbohydrate 59g (Dietary Fiber 14g; Sugars 7g); Protein 24g

% Daily Value: Vitamin A 20%; Vitamin C 30%; Calcium 25%; Iron 30%

Exchanges: 4 Starch, 1 1/2 Lean Meat

Carbohydrate Choices: 3

4

STEADY COOKING WITH THE SLOW COOKER

Garden Harvest Chicken Soup

Prep Time: 25 Minutes   **Start to Finish:** 7 Hours 45 Minutes

6 servings (1 1/3 cups each)

note from the nutritionist:

Soup is soothing to the body as well as to the soul, and this is a great choice because it contains lots of vitamin A, vitamin C and iron from the chicken and vegetables. Pair this delicious soup with Parmesan-Sesame Breadsticks (page 82) or any soft breadsticks.

1 lb boneless skinless chicken thighs, cut into 3/4-inch pieces

1 teaspoon peppered seasoned salt

2 medium unpeeled red potatoes, cut into 1/2-inch pieces (2 cups)

2 medium carrots, sliced (1 cup)

1 medium onion, coarsely chopped (1/2 cup)

2 cans (14 oz each) chicken broth

2 cups small broccoli flowerets

1 medium yellow summer squash, coarsely chopped (1 1/2 cups)

2 tablespoons chopped fresh basil leaves

1. Heat 10-inch nonstick skillet over medium-high heat. Add chicken to skillet; sprinkle with peppered seasoned salt. Cook 6 to 8 minutes, stirring occasionally, until brown.

2. In 3 1/2- to 4-quart slow cooker, mix chicken, potatoes, carrots, onion and broth.

3. Cover and cook on Low heat setting 7 to 8 hours.

4. Stir in broccoli, squash and basil. Increase heat setting to High. Cover and cook 15 to 20 minutes or until vegetables are tender.

1 Serving: Calories 200 (Calories from Fat 60); Total Fat 7g (Saturated Fat 2g); Cholesterol 45mg; Sodium 850mg; Total Carbohydrate 16g (Dietary Fiber 4g; Sugars 3g); Protein 21g

% Daily Value: Vitamin A 90%; Vitamin C 35%; Calcium 6%; Iron 15%

Exchanges: 1/2 Starch, 1 Vegetable, 2 1/2 Lean Meat

Carbohydrate Choices: 1

Split Pea Soup

8 servings (1 1/2 cups each)

7 cups water

1 package (16 oz) dried split peas
(2 1/4 cups), sorted, rinsed

1 teaspoon salt

1/4 teaspoon pepper

3 medium carrots, cut into
1/4-inch slices (1 1/2 cups)

2 medium stalks celery,
finely chopped (1 cup)

1 medium onion, chopped (1/2 cup)

1 ham bone, 2 lb ham shanks or
2 lb smoked pork hocks

1. In 4- to 5-quart slow cooker, mix all ingredients except ham. Add ham.

2. Cover and cook on Low heat setting 8 to 10 hours.

3. Remove ham from cooker; place on cutting board. Pull meat from bones, using 2 forks; discard bones and skin. Stir ham into soup. Stir well before serving.

note from the nutritionist:

Dried peas, beans and lentils are loaded with fiber, vitamins and minerals and are an excellent ingredient in soups and stews. Look for split peas with the dried beans and lentils in your supermarket.

*My dad's a great tennis player—
I'm still learning. He's always fair with me,
and I love to hit balls with him.*

Elizabeth H. age 8

1 Serving: Calories 190
(Calories from Fat 60); Total Fat 6g
(Saturated Fat 2g); Cholesterol
15mg; Sodium 550mg;
Total Carbohydrate 33g (Dietary
Fiber 16g; Sugars 3g); Protein 16g

% Daily Value: Vitamin A 90%;
Vitamin C 4%; Calcium 4%;
Iron 10%

Exchanges: 2 Starch, 1 1/2 Very
Lean Meat, 1 Fat

Carbohydrate Choices: 1

Tuscan Bean and Ham Soup

Prep Time: **20 Minutes**   Start to Finish: **8 Hours 20 Minutes**

6 servings (1 1/2 cups each)

1 lb small red potatoes, cut into fourths (about 3 cups)

4 medium carrots, sliced (2 cups)

1 medium onion, chopped (1/2 cup)

2 cloves garlic, finely chopped

2 cans (15 to 16 oz each) great northern beans, rinsed, drained

1 can (14 oz) chicken broth

1 cup water

1 1/2 cups diced fully cooked ham

1 teaspoon Italian seasoning

2 tablespoons chopped fresh parsley

1 tablespoon olive or canola oil

1. In 3- to 4-quart slow cooker, mix all ingredients except parsley and oil.

2. Cover and cook on Low heat setting 8 to 10 hours.

3. Stir in parsley and oil.

1 Serving: Calories 320 (Calories from Fat 60); Total Fat 6g (Saturated Fat 1.5g); Cholesterol 20mg; Sodium 810mg; Total Carbohydrate 50g (Dietary Fiber 11g; Sugars 4g); Protein 23g

% Daily Value: Vitamin A 150%; Vitamin C 15%; Calcium 15%; Iron 40%

Exchanges: 3 Starch, 2 Very Lean Meat, 1/2 Fat

Carbohydrate Choices: 2 1/2

Beef-Barley Soup

Prep Time: 10 Minutes   **Start to Finish:** 8 Hours 20 Minutes

6 servings (1 1/3 cups each)

1 1/2 lb boneless beef round steak, cut into 1 1/2-inch cubes

2 medium carrots, sliced (1 cup)

1 medium onion, chopped (1/2 cup)

1 cup sliced fresh mushrooms (3 oz)

3 cans (14 oz each) beef broth

1 cup water

1/2 cup uncooked barley

2 dried bay leaves

1 cup frozen baby sweet peas (from 1-lb bag)

1. In 4- to 5-quart slow cooker, mix all ingredients except peas.

2. Cover and cook on Low heat setting 8 to 9 hours.

3. About 10 minutes before serving, stir in peas. Increase heat setting to High. Cover and cook about 10 minutes or until peas are cooked through. Remove bay leaves.

note from DR. H:

Need some motivation? Learn about the benefits of exercise, and keep that info in mind as you are working out. Knowing how your dedication and hard work will pay off will help you get going and keep going.

My mom got my dad and me to go for a walk with her. At first I thought it would be lame to walk around with my parents, but we talk about lots of things that we might not if I was watching TV.

Carlon O. age 14

1 Serving: Calories 240 (Calories from Fat 35); Total Fat 4g (Saturated Fat 1.5g); Cholesterol 60mg; Sodium 840mg; Total Carbohydrate 22g (Dietary Fiber 4g; Sugars 4g); Protein 33g

% Daily Value: Vitamin A 80%; Vitamin C 6%; Calcium 4%; Iron 20%

Exchanges: 1 Starch, 1 Vegetable, 4 Very Lean Meat

Carbohydrate Choices: 1 1/2

Beef-Vegetable Chili

Prep Time: 20 Minutes   **Start to Finish:** 7 Hours 20 Minutes

6 servings (1 1/2 cups each)

note from DR. H:

Do you drink enough water? At least eight to ten glasses of water and other liquids are recommended daily. Skim milk and herb teas count, too, but remember to quench your thirst with plenty of fresh plain water.

1 1/2 lb boneless beef round steak, cut into 1/2-inch cubes

1 large onion, coarsely chopped (1 cup)

2 cups frozen mixed vegetables (from 1-lb bag), thawed

2 cans (14.5 oz each) diced tomatoes with green chilies, undrained

1 can (15 oz) black beans, rinsed, drained

1 can (15 to 16 oz) dark red kidney beans, rinsed, drained

1 package (1.25 oz) chili seasoning mix

2 cups water

3/4 cup shredded Cheddar cheese (3 oz)

2 tablespoons chopped fresh cilantro

1. Heat 12-inch nonstick skillet over medium-high heat. Cook beef and onion in skillet 7 to 9 minutes, stirring occasionally, until beef is brown; drain.

2. In 3 1/2- to 4-quart slow cooker, mix beef mixture and remaining ingredients except cheese and cilantro.

3. Cover and cook on Low heat setting 7 to 9 hours. Top individual servings with cheese and cilantro.

1 Serving: Calories 420 (Calories from Fat 90); Total Fat 10g (Saturated Fat 4.5g); Cholesterol 75mg; Sodium 950mg; Total Carbohydrate 50g (Dietary Fiber 14g; Sugars 9g); Protein 41g

% Daily Value: Vitamin A 80%; Vitamin C 20%; Calcium 20%; Iron 150%

Exchanges: 3 Starch, 1 Vegetable, 4 Lean Meat

Carbohydrate Choices: 2 1/2

I always keep a water bottle in my backpack for after recess or whenever I am thirsty at school.

Ruby O. age 9

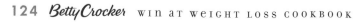

Family-Favorite Pot Roast

Prep Time: 25 Minutes **Start to Finish: 8 Hours 40 Minutes**

6 servings

2 teaspoons olive or canola oil

2- to 2 1/2-lb beef bottom round roast

6 medium potatoes, cut into 2-inch pieces (about 4 cups)

2 1/2 cups baby-cut carrots

2 cups sliced fresh mushrooms (about 5 oz)

1 medium stalk celery, sliced (1/2 cup)

1 medium onion, chopped (1/2 cup)

1 teaspoon salt

1/2 teaspoon pepper

1/2 teaspoon dried thyme leaves

1 can (14.5 oz) diced tomatoes, undrained

1 can (10 1/2 oz) condensed beef consommé or broth

1 can (5.5 oz) eight-vegetable juice (2/3 cup)

1/4 cup all-purpose flour

1. In 10-inch skillet, heat oil over medium-high heat. If beef roast comes in netting or is tied, do not remove. Cook beef in oil about 10 minutes, turning occasionally, until brown on all sides.

2. In 4- to 5-quart slow cooker, place potatoes, carrots, mushrooms, celery and onion. Sprinkle with salt, pepper and thyme. Place beef on vegetables. Pour tomatoes, consommé and vegetable juice over beef.

3. Cover and cook on Low heat setting 8 to 10 hours.

4. Remove beef and vegetables from cooker, using slotted spoon; place on serving platter and cover to keep warm. Skim fat from beef juices in cooker. Remove 1/2 cup of the juices from cooker; in small bowl, mix juices and flour, using wire whisk, until smooth. Gradually stir flour mixture into remaining juices in cooker. Increase heat setting to High. Cover and cook about 15 minutes or until thickened. Remove netting or strings from beef. Serve sauce with beef and vegetables.

note from DR. H:

Slow cooking is a great way to cook because not much added fat is needed. It also helps you plan ahead, and you can combine meats, veggies and other good-for-you foods. More good news—dinner is ready when you walk in the door, so why not take the time for a bit of extra activity?

1 Serving: Calories 330 (Calories from Fat 60); Total Fat 7g (Saturated Fat 2g); Cholesterol 80mg; Sodium 920mg; Total Carbohydrate 35g (Dietary Fiber 6g; Sugars 7g); Protein 37g

% Daily Value: Vitamin A 200%; Vitamin C 30%; Calcium 8%; Iron 35%

Exchanges: 1 1/2 Starch, 1 1/2 Vegetable, 4 Lean Meat

Carbohydrate Choices: 2

Salsa Swiss Steak with Noodles

Prep Time: 10 Minutes   **Start to Finish:** 8 Hours 10 Minutes

9 servings

3-lb boneless beef round steak, cut into 9 serving pieces

1 jar (16 oz) thick-and-chunky salsa

1 package (0.87 oz) brown gravy mix

1 bag (16 oz) frozen home-style egg noodles

1. In 3- to 4-quart slow cooker, place beef pieces. In small bowl, mix salsa and gravy mix; pour over beef.

2. Cover and cook on Low heat setting 8 to 10 hours.

3. About 15 minutes before serving, cook and drain noodles as directed on package. Serve beef and sauce over noodles.

note from the nutritionist:

Talk about easy: only three ingredients that cook during the day, then you make the noodles, and dinner is ready. Mix it up by serving this southwestern steak dinner with long-grain brown rice instead of noodles.

1 Serving: Calories 250 (Calories from Fat 50); Total Fat 6g (Saturated Fat 2g); Cholesterol 95mg; Sodium 500mg; Total Carbohydrate 17g (Dietary Fiber 1g; Sugars 2g); Protein 33g

% Daily Value: Vitamin A 8%; Vitamin C 6%; Calcium 4%; Iron 25%

Exchanges: 1 Starch, 4 Lean Meat

Carbohydrate Choices: 1

We have really reduced the sodas. To help make the transition easier, we drank a lot of flavored non-carbonated waters. We use non-sugar sweetened ones and that saves at least 100 sugar calories per drink.

Deb M.

Tex-Mex Steak and Rice

Prep Time: 10 Minutes   Start to Finish: 7 Hours 40 Minutes

4 servings

1 1/4 lb boneless beef round, tip or chuck steak, about 3/4 inch thick

1 cup beef broth

1 can (14.5 oz) Southwestern salsa-style diced tomatoes with green chilies, undrained

2 teaspoons ground cumin

2 cloves garlic, finely chopped

2 cups frozen stir-fry bell peppers and onions (from 1-lb bag), thawed, drained

1 cup uncooked instant rice

1. Cut beef steak into 4 serving pieces; place in 3- to 4-quart slow cooker. In medium bowl, mix broth, tomatoes, cumin and garlic; pour over beef.

2. Cover and cook on Low heat setting 7 to 8 hours.

3. Stir bell pepper mixture and rice into mixture in cooker. Increase heat setting to High. Cover and cook 20 to 30 minutes or until rice is tender.

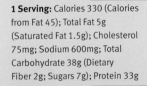

note from the nutritionist:

The moist heat of a slow cooker transforms inexpensive, less-tender cuts of meat into a fork-tender dinner. Be sure to choose the leanest cuts of beef: round, tip or chuck steak. Get a fiber boost by using instant brown rice instead of the white rice.

When the kids get off the school bus, I have their favorite fruit ready and waiting for them. That way they won't be looking around for cookies and sweet snacks.

Steve O.

1 Serving: Calories 330 (Calories from Fat 45); Total Fat 5g (Saturated Fat 1.5g); Cholesterol 75mg; Sodium 600mg; Total Carbohydrate 38g (Dietary Fiber 2g; Sugars 7g); Protein 33g

% Daily Value: Vitamin A 10%; Vitamin C 35%; Calcium 6%; Iron 30%

Exchanges: 1 1/2 Starch, 1/2 Other Carbohydrate, 1 Vegetable, 3 1/2 Very Lean Meat, 1/2 Fat

Carbohydrate Choices: 2 1/2

Italian Smothered Steak

Prep Time: 10 Minutes   **Start to Finish:** 8 Hours 30 Minutes

6 servings

2 lb boneless beef round steak

1/2 teaspoon seasoned salt

1/4 teaspoon pepper

1 medium onion, sliced

1 jar (26 oz) tomato pasta sauce (any variety)

1 package (9 oz) refrigerated cheese-filled tortellini

1 medium zucchini, cut lengthwise in half, then cut crosswise into slices (about 1 cup)

1. Cut beef into 6 serving-size pieces; sprinkle with seasoned salt and pepper. In 3- to 4-quart slow cooker, layer beef and onion. Pour pasta sauce over top.

2. Cover and cook on Low heat setting 8 to 9 hours.

3. About 20 minutes before serving, stir in tortellini and zucchini. Increase heat setting to High. Cover and cook 15 to 20 minutes or until tortellini are tender.

1 Serving: Calories 360 (Calories from Fat 100); Total Fat 11g (Saturated Fat 3.5g); Cholesterol 115mg; Sodium 800mg; Total Carbohydrate 32g (Dietary Fiber 3g; Sugars 10g); Protein 35g

% Daily Value: Vitamin A 20%; Vitamin C 20%; Calcium 8%; Iron 25%

Exchanges: 1 Starch, 1 Other Carbohydrate, 4 1/2 Lean Meat

Carbohydrate Choices: 2

Italian Smothered Steak

Cheeseburger Sandwiches

Prep Time: 20 Minutes   **Start to Finish:** 6 Hours 20 Minutes

12 sandwiches

1 1/2 lb extra-lean (at least 90%) ground beef

1/2 teaspoon garlic-pepper seasoning

1/2 package (8-oz size) pasteurized prepared cheese product loaf, diced (1 cup)

2 tablespoons fat-free (skim) milk

1 medium green bell pepper, chopped (1 cup)

1 small onion, chopped (1/4 cup)

2 cloves garlic, finely chopped

12 whole wheat sandwich buns, split

1. In 12-inch skillet, cook beef and garlic-pepper seasoning over medium heat 8 to 10 minutes, stirring occasionally, until beef is brown; drain.

2. Spray 3- to 4-quart slow cooker with cooking spray. Mix beef and remaining ingredients except buns in cooker.

3. Cover and cook on Low heat setting 6 to 7 hours. To serve, fill buns with beef mixture.

1 Sandwich: Calories 230 (Calories from Fat 90); Total Fat 10g (Saturated Fat 5g); Cholesterol 50mg; Sodium 500mg; Total Carbohydrate 20g (Dietary Fiber 3g; Sugars 6g); Protein 18g

% Daily Value: Vitamin A 6%; Vitamin C 8%; Calcium 15%; Iron 15%

Exchanges: 1 1/2 Starch, 2 Medium-Fat Meat

Carbohydrate Choices: 1

Sausage Pizza Sloppy Joes

Prep Time: 25 Minutes **Start to Finish:** 4 Hours 25 Minutes

18 sandwiches

1 1/2 lb bulk Italian sausage

2 cups frozen stir-fry bell peppers and onions (from 1-lb bag), thawed

1 can (15 oz) pizza sauce

1/2 teaspoon Italian seasoning

3 plum (Roma) tomatoes, coarsely chopped (1 cup)

18 sandwich buns

1 1/4 cups shredded part-skim mozzarella cheese (5 oz)

1. In 10-inch skillet, cook sausage over medium-high heat 9 to 11 minutes, stirring occasionally, until no longer pink; drain.

2. Spray 3- to 4-quart slow cooker with cooking spray. Mix sausage, stir-fry vegetables, pizza sauce and Italian seasoning in cooker.

3. Cover and cook on Low heat setting 4 to 6 hours.

4. Stir in tomatoes. To serve, fill buns with sausage mixture and sprinkle with cheese.

note from the nutritionist:

Super-easy and a hit with adults and kids alike, this recipe is a great choice for a healthy totable meal when you are serving lots of people or a crowd. Just bring your slow cooker with the filling, tote the whole wheat buns and cheese, and you're set.

1 Sandwich: Calories 250 (Calories from Fat 100); Total Fat 11g (Saturated Fat 4g); Cholesterol 25mg; Sodium 680mg; Total Carbohydrate 26g (Dietary Fiber 2g; Sugars 3g); Protein 12g

% Daily Value: Vitamin A 6%; Vitamin C 10%; Calcium 15%; Iron 10%

Exchanges: 1 1/2 Starch, 1 High-Fat Meat, 1/2 Fat

Carbohydrate Choices: 2

Chile-Chicken Tacos

Prep Time: 15 Minutes   **Start to Finish:** 6 Hours 30 Minutes

6 servings (2 tacos each)

note from DR. H:

The hardest part of beginning to exercise is getting started. As you get used to exercise being a part of your life, you become stronger and leaner and likely to feel more energized, a motivator to keep you going.

1 1/4 lb boneless skinless chicken thighs

1 package (1.25 oz) taco seasoning mix

1 tablespoon packed brown sugar

1 can (4.5 oz) chopped green chiles, undrained

1 cup frozen whole-kernel corn (from 1-lb bag), thawed

1 can (10 oz) enchilada sauce

4 medium green onions, sliced (1/4 cup)

1 package (4.6 oz) taco shells, warmed if desired

3 cups shredded lettuce

1 medium tomato, chopped (3/4 cup)

1. Spray 3- to 4-quart slow cooker with cooking spray; add chicken thighs. Sprinkle with taco seasoning mix and brown sugar; toss to coat. Mix in green chiles, corn and 1/2 cup of the enchilada sauce. Refrigerate remaining enchilada sauce.

2. Cover and cook on Low heat setting 6 to 7 hours.

3. Remove chicken from cooker; place on cutting board. Use 2 forks to pull chicken into shreds. Return chicken to cooker. Stir in green onions. Cover and cook on Low heat setting 15 minutes.

4. Heat remaining enchilada sauce. Serve chicken mixture in taco shells with lettuce, tomato and warm enchilada sauce.

1 Serving: Calories 320 (Calories from Fat 120); Total Fat 13g (Saturated Fat 3g); Cholesterol 60mg; Sodium 900mg; Total Carbohydrate 31g (Dietary Fiber 5g; Sugars 9g); Protein 24g

% Daily Value: Vitamin A 30%; Vitamin C 15%; Calcium 10%; Iron 20%

Exchanges: 2 Starch, 2 1/2 Lean Meat, 1 Fat

Carbohydrate Choices: 2

Bouncing up and down on the exercise ball is fun!
Ruby O. age 9

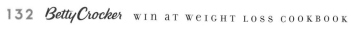

Chile-Chicken Tacos

Slow-Cooked Pork Burrito Bowls

Prep Time: 15 Minutes   Start to Finish: 8 Hours 15 Minutes

10 servings

2-lb boneless pork shoulder roast

1 can (15 to 16 oz) pinto beans, rinsed, drained

2 tablespoons taco seasoning mix (from 1.25-oz package)

1 can (4.5 oz) diced green chiles, undrained

2 packages (7.6 oz each) Spanish rice mix

5 cups water

1 tablespoon butter or margarine

1 1/2 cups shredded Mexican blend cheese (6 oz)

2 1/4 cups shredded lettuce

1/2 cup thick-and-chunky salsa

1. If pork roast comes in netting or is tied, remove netting or strings. In 3- to 4-quart slow cooker, place pork. Pour beans around pork. Sprinkle taco seasoning mix over pork. Pour green chiles over beans.

2. Cover and cook on Low heat setting 8 to 10 hours.

3. About 45 minutes before serving, in 3-quart saucepan, make rice mixes as directed on package, using water and butter.

4. Remove pork from cooker; place on cutting board. Use 2 forks to pull pork into shreds. Return pork to cooker; gently stir to mix with beans.

5. To serve, spoon rice into each serving bowl and top with pork mixture, cheese, lettuce and salsa.

1 Serving: Calories 450 (Calories from Fat 160); Total Fat 18g (Saturated Fat 8g); Cholesterol 75mg; Sodium 1050mg; Total Carbohydrate 46g (Dietary Fiber 5g; Sugars 4g); Protein 30g

% Daily Value: Vitamin A 15%; Vitamin C 15%; Calcium 20%; Iron 20%

Exchanges: 3 Starch, 3 Lean Meat, 1 1/2 Fat

Carbohydrate Choices: 3

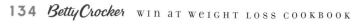

Slow-Cooked Pork Burrito Bowls

Pork Chops with Cheesy Corn Bread Stuffing

Prep Time: 15 Minutes   Start to Finish: 5 Hours 15 Minutes

6 servings

note from the nutritionist:

Instead of the boneless chops, you can use lean bone-in pork loin chops. Before cooking, just be sure to trim any excess fat.

6 boneless pork loin chops, about 3/4 inch thick (2 lb)

1 teaspoon peppered seasoned salt

1/2 bag (16-oz size) corn bread stuffing mix (3 cups)

1 medium onion, chopped (1/2 cup)

1/2 cup chopped red or green bell pepper

1/2 teaspoon dried thyme leaves

1 1/4 cups water

1/2 cup finely shredded Cheddar cheese (2 oz)

1. Sprinkle pork chops with peppered seasoned salt. Spray 10-inch skillet with cooking spray; heat over medium heat. Cook pork in skillet 5 to 6 minutes, turning occasionally, until brown on both sides.

2. Spray 3 1/2- to 4-quart slow cooker with cooking spray. Mix remaining ingredients except cheese in cooker. Arrange pork on stuffing, layering as necessary.

3. Cover and cook on Low heat setting 5 to 6 hours.

4. Remove pork from cooker. Stir cheese into stuffing in cooker until melted. Serve pork with stuffing.

1 Serving: Calories 390 (Calories from Fat 140); Total Fat 16g (Saturated Fat 6g); Cholesterol 105mg; Sodium 660mg; Total Carbohydrate 25g (Dietary Fiber 2g; Sugars 4g); Protein 38g

% Daily Value: Vitamin A 15%; Vitamin C 20%; Calcium 10%; Iron 15%

Exchanges: 1 1/2 Starch, 4 1/2 Lean Meat, 1/2 Fat

Carbohydrate Choices: 1 1/2

Slowly step your way into weight reduction. In order to reach 10,000 steps a day, I have to walk 4,000 to 5,000 steps before I even get to work. Once at work, it's been helpful to take at least one walking break and join a lunchtime walking group.

Greg S.

Barbecued Beans and Sausage

Prep Time: 10 Minutes   **Start to Finish:** 5 Hours 10 Minutes

12 servings

2 cans (15 to 16 oz each) great northern beans, rinsed, drained

2 cans (15 oz each) black beans, rinsed, drained

1 large onion, chopped (1 cup)

1 cup barbecue sauce

1/4 cup packed brown sugar

1 tablespoon ground mustard

1 tablespoon Worcestershire sauce

2 teaspoons chili powder

1 ring (1 lb) fully cooked turkey smoked sausage or 1 ring (14 oz) fully cooked turkey kielbasa

1. Spray 3- to 4-quart slow cooker with cooking spray. Mix all ingredients except sausage in cooker. Place sausage ring on bean mixture.

2. Cover and cook on Low heat setting 5 to 6 hours.

note from the nutritionist:

Using turkey sausage in place of full-fat sausage helps you cut the fat— but not the taste—in this family-friendly recipe by over half. Serve hearty whole-grain or dark bread such as pumpernickel and sliced crisp apples to complement the barbecue flavor.

1 Serving: Calories 270 (Calories from Fat 40); Total Fat 4g (Saturated Fat 1g); Cholesterol 20mg; Sodium 840mg; Total Carbohydrate 45g (Dietary Fiber 8g; Sugars 13g); Protein 17g

% Daily Value: Vitamin A 4%; Vitamin C 2%; Calcium 10%; Iron 25%

Exchanges: 2 Starch, 1 Other Carbohydrate, 1 1/2 Lean Meat

Carbohydrate Choices: 2 1/2

Feeding Your Emotions

Do you reach for snacks during a stressful day even though you may not be hungry? Do you crave ice cream or potato chips late at night even when your stomach isn't rumbling? If so, you may be an emotional eater.

Emotional eating is the urge to eat in order to satisfy a feeling rather than physical hunger. Our bodies give us gradual physiological cues, such as a sense of emptiness, lightheadedness or low energy, when it's time to eat. But emotional hunger is often sudden and specific. If you have an urgent desire for pizza or ice cream after a tough day at work, your craving is likely triggered by emotions.

Common triggers for emotional hunger include stress, depression, sadness, anger, loneliness, boredom and fatigue. Using food to alleviate these feelings might make you feel better now, but it doesn't fix the underlying issue. Emotional eating also adds calories your body may not need and can cause you to feel bad about yourself later.

Know Your Triggers

To break bad habits, you first have to identify them. If you suspect you're an emotional eater, start paying attention to when and why you eat. Ask yourself these important questions whenever you reach for a snack:

Are you truly hungry?

Are you eating because it's time for breakfast/lunch/dinner?

Are you eating to give yourself an energy boost or because you need to soothe yourself after a rough day?

What emotions are you currently experiencing?

After several days, you may begin to see a pattern emerge. Make a list of the feelings most likely to trigger emotional eating for you.

Change Your Routine

The next step is finding other ways to deal with these triggers and keep your mind off cravings until physical hunger returns. Start with these ideas:

If you snack while watching late-night TV, spend time on a hobby or drink a soothing blend of herbal tea instead of snacking.

If boredom or loneliness is a trigger for you, take a class, join a book club or connect with a friend.

If your hand reaches for food when you're angry, write down the reasons you are upset, discuss the situation with a friend or work toward resolving the source of your frustration.

If stress is your hot button, start a new physical activity: go for a walk, take a warm bath and stick to a regular sleep pattern.

If you feel compelled to eat, try substituting healthier snacks for high-fat comfort foods or limit your portions. You may also need to change your routine to avoid a social situation or deal with a time of day that triggers emotional eating.

As you work on curbing your cravings, remember to set reasonable goals and reward yourself for staying on track. When you learn to manage the impulses, you will be happier—and healthier.

Mediterranean Minestrone Casserole

Prep Time: 15 Minutes   Start to Finish: 6 Hours 35 Minutes

5 servings

3 medium carrots, sliced (1 1/2 cups)

1 medium onion, chopped (1/2 cup)

1 cup water

2 teaspoons sugar

1 teaspoon Italian seasoning

1/4 teaspoon pepper

1 can (28 oz) diced tomatoes, undrained

1 can (15 to 16 oz) garbanzo beans, rinsed, drained

1 can (6 oz) Italian-style tomato paste

2 cloves garlic, finely chopped

1 1/2 cups frozen cut green beans (from 1-lb bag), thawed

1 cup uncooked elbow macaroni (3 1/2 oz)

1/2 cup shredded Parmesan cheese (2 oz)

1. In 3- to 4-quart slow cooker, mix all ingredients except green beans, macaroni and cheese.

2. Cover and cook on Low heat setting 6 to 8 hours.

3. Stir in green beans and macaroni. Increase heat setting to High. Cover and cook about 20 minutes or until beans and macaroni are tender. Sprinkle with cheese.

note from DR. H:

Looking for a healthy dose of vegetables? This meatless main dish has carrots, onions, tomatoes and green beans, in addition to fiber-rich garbanzos. Just one serving of this casserole gives you all the vitamin A and one-third of the iron and calcium you need for the whole day.

We tried eating one vegetarian meal each week. Then we tried two, then three. Before we knew it, we were only eating meat once or twice a week.

Alyson S.

1 Serving: Calories 320 (Calories from Fat 50); Total Fat 6g (Saturated Fat 2g); Cholesterol 10mg; Sodium 810mg; Total Carbohydrate 59g (Dietary Fiber 11g; Sugars 10g); Protein 17g

% Daily Value: Vitamin A 160%; Vitamin C 35%; Calcium 25%; Iron 30%

Exchanges: 3 Starch, 1/2 Other Carbohydrate, 1 Vegetable, 1/2 Very Lean Meat, 1 Fat

Carbohydrate Choices: 3

FAMILY-PLEASING FISH, POULTRY and MEAT

Corn Flake–Crusted Fish Fillets

Prep Time: 30 Minutes   Start to Finish: 30 Minutes

4 servings

1/2 cup all-purpose flour

1/2 teaspoon salt

1 egg

1/4 cup water

3 cups Country® Corn Flakes cereal, crushed (about 1 2/3 cups)

4 cod fillets (4 to 6 oz each)

2 tablespoons canola or soybean oil

1. In shallow dish, mix flour and salt. In another shallow dish, beat egg and water with fork. Place crushed cereal in third shallow dish. Dip fish in flour, coating well; shake off excess. Dip floured fish in egg mixture, then in cereal, coating all sides completely. Place coated fish on ungreased cookie sheet.

2. In 12-inch nonstick skillet, heat oil over medium heat until hot. Keeping at least 1 inch between fish fillets and cooking in batches if needed, cook fish in oil 3 to 4 minutes on each side, turning once, until well browned and fish flakes easily with fork. If needed, place cooked fish on paper towels on cookie sheet and keep warm in 225°F oven while cooking remaining fish.

note from the nutritionist:

Using whole-grain cereals as a breading or in baking is an easy way to work in whole grains and boosts vitamins and minerals in your favorite recipes, because the cereal is fortified. You can pair these crispy fillets with seasoned rice pilaf, coleslaw and baby carrots.

1 Serving: Calories 320 (Calories from Fat 90); Total Fat 10g (Saturated Fat 1.5g); Cholesterol 115mg; Sodium 600mg; Total Carbohydrate 31g (Dietary Fiber 0g; Sugars 2g); Protein 26g

% Daily Value: Vitamin A 10%; Vitamin C 4%; Calcium 20%; Iron 40%

Exchanges: 2 Starch, 3 Very Lean Meat, 1 1/2 Fat

Carbohydrate Choices: 2.

Tuna Tetrazzini

Prep Time: 15 Minutes **Start to Finish:** 1 Hour 5 Minutes

5 servings

8 oz uncooked spaghetti, broken into 2-inch pieces

1 can (12 oz) chunk light tuna in water, drained

1/4 cup fat-free (skim) milk

1 jar (1 lb) reduced-fat Alfredo pasta sauce

1 jar (4.5 oz) sliced mushrooms, drained

1 cup frozen sweet peas (from 1-lb bag), thawed

1 jar (2 oz) diced pimientos, drained

2 tablespoons grated Parmesan cheese

1. Heat oven to 350°F. Cook and drain spaghetti as directed on package.

2. Meanwhile, in ungreased 2-quart casserole, stir tuna, milk, Alfredo sauce, mushrooms, peas and pimientos. Gently stir in cooked spaghetti.

3. Cover and bake 40 minutes. Sprinkle cheese over top. Bake uncovered about 10 minutes longer or until top is bubbly and beginning to brown.

note from the nutritionist:

This recipe is an excellent source of iron and calcium, thanks to the pasta, tuna and milk. Look for recipes that have a high amount of these minerals, because many kids do not get enough calcium and iron and it's so important for short-term and long-term good health.

We started walking to school this year. It is 1.5 miles to the school, so it is 3 miles a day for the kids and 6 for me. Even my petite 6-year-old enjoys it.

Deb M.

1 Serving: Calories 420 (Calories from Fat 110); Total Fat 12g (Saturated Fat 7g); Cholesterol 55mg; Sodium 990mg; Total Carbohydrate 50g (Dietary Fiber 4g; Sugars 6g); Protein 31g

% Daily Value: Vitamin A 15%; Vitamin C 6%; Calcium 25%; Iron 20%

Exchanges: 3 Starch, 3 Very Lean Meat, 2 Fat

Carbohydrate Choices: 3

Halibut with Potato Succotash

Prep Time: 20 Minutes   Start to Finish: 45 Minutes

4 servings

note from the nutritionist:

Halibut is a good source of protein and is particularly low in saturated fat, but you can use any fish you like. If your family enjoys the taste of salmon, that's a good choice for this delicious dish.

1-lb halibut fillet

2 tablespoons butter or margarine

2 cups frozen potatoes O'Brien with onions and peppers (from 28-oz bag)

1 box (9 oz) frozen baby lima beans

1 cup frozen whole-kernel corn (from 1-lb bag)

1/2 teaspoon garlic-pepper seasoning

1/2 teaspoon seasoned salt

1/2 teaspoon dried thyme leaves

1/8 teaspoon ground red pepper (cayenne)

1. Heat oven to 425°F. Spray 11x7-inch (2-quart) glass baking dish with cooking spray. Cut halibut into 4 serving-size pieces; place in baking dish. Melt 1 tablespoon of the butter; brush over halibut.

2. In 10-inch nonstick skillet, melt remaining 1 tablespoon butter over medium-high heat. Cook potatoes in butter 5 minutes, stirring occasionally. Stir in lima beans and corn. Cook 3 to 5 minutes or until vegetables are crisp-tender. Spoon mixture around halibut in baking dish. Sprinkle halibut and vegetables with remaining ingredients; stir vegetables slightly.

3. Bake uncovered 20 to 25 minutes or until halibut flakes easily with fork and vegetables are tender.

1 Serving: Calories 310 (Calories from Fat 70); Total Fat 8g (Saturated Fat 3.5g); Cholesterol 75mg; Sodium 400mg; Total Carbohydrate 37g (Dietary Fiber 6g; Sugars 2g); Protein 28g

% Daily Value: Vitamin A 10%; Vitamin C 20%; Calcium 4%; Iron 10%

Exchanges: 2 1/2 Starch, 3 Very Lean Meat, 1 Fat

Carbohydrate Choices: 2

Halibut with Potato Succotash

Bow-Ties and Shrimp Casserole

Prep Time: 15 Minutes   **Start to Finish:** 1 Hour

5 servings

3 cups uncooked bow-tie (farfalle) pasta (6 oz)

3 tablespoons leek soup, dip and recipe mix (half of 1.8-oz package)

2 cups fat-free (skim) milk

1 lb cooked peeled deveined medium shrimp, thawed if frozen and tails peeled

1 1/2 cups frozen baby peas (from 1-lb bag)

1/2 cup shredded Havarti cheese (2 oz)

1/4 teaspoon paprika

1. Heat oven to 350°F. Spray 2-quart casserole with cooking spray. Cook and drain pasta as directed on package. Place pasta in casserole.

2. In same saucepan, heat soup mix and milk over medium heat just to boiling, stirring constantly. Pour over pasta. Add shrimp and peas to casserole; stir gently to mix. Sprinkle with cheese and paprika.

3. Cover and bake 35 to 45 minutes or until thoroughly heated and bubbly around edges.

note from the nutritionist:

Make a commitment to healthy eating: switch to lower-fat dairy products like fat-free milk and reduced-fat cheese, cottage cheese and yogurts. Some cheeses, like Havarti, do not come in reduced-fat form, but you can cut fat by just using less.

1 Serving: Calories 290 (Calories from Fat 60); Total Fat 6g (Saturated Fat 3.5g); Cholesterol 215mg; Sodium 840mg; Total Carbohydrate 30g (Dietary Fiber 2g; Sugars 8g); Protein 30g

% Daily Value: Vitamin A 20%; Vitamin C 8%; Calcium 25%; Iron 25%

Exchanges: 2 Starch, 3 1/2 Very Lean Meat, 1/2 Fat

Carbohydrate Choices: 2

I head for the gym first thing in the morning 3 days a week to exercise. That way, I get my workout done before anything can interfere with it, and I feel good all day.

Cheri O.

Nutty Salmon and Rice

Prep Time: 15 Minutes   Start to Finish: 1 Hour 5 Minutes

4 servings

1 package (6 oz) original-flavor long grain and wild rice mix

1/4 cup chopped pecans

1 1/2 cups water

1- to 1 1/2-lb salmon fillet

2 tablespoons orange marmalade

2 teaspoons soy sauce

1/4 teaspoon ground ginger

1/4 cup chopped fresh parsley

1. Heat oven to 400°F. Spray 11x7-inch (2-quart) glass baking dish with cooking spray. In baking dish, mix rice, seasoning packet from rice mix, pecans and water.

2. Remove skin from salmon with sharp knife. Cut salmon into 4 serving-size pieces; place on rice mixture. In small bowl, mix marmalade, soy sauce and ginger; brush over salmon. Cover baking dish with foil.

3. Bake 40 to 50 minutes or until salmon flakes easily with fork and rice is tender. Sprinkle with parsley.

note from the nutritionist:

Salmon is an excellent source of omega-3 fatty acids, nutrients that may reduce the risk of heart disease. For that reason and because people who eat more fish tend to eat less saturated fat overall, nutrition experts recommend serving fish once or twice every week.

1 Serving: Calories 410 (Calories from Fat 110); Total Fat 12g (Saturated Fat 2.5g); Cholesterol 75mg; Sodium 590mg; Total Carbohydrate 46g (Dietary Fiber 2g; Sugars 6g); Protein 31g

% Daily Value: Vitamin A 10%; Vitamin C 6%; Calcium 4%; Iron 15%

Exchanges: 3 Starch, 3 Lean Meat

Carbohydrate Choices: 3

Turkey and Corn Bread Casserole

Prep Time: 25 Minutes   Start to Finish: 1 Hour 40 Minutes

6 servings

2 tablespoons butter or margarine

1 medium onion, chopped (1/2 cup)

1 small red bell pepper, chopped (1/2 cup)

4 cups seasoned corn bread stuffing mix

1 cup frozen whole-kernel corn (from 1-lb bag)

1 1/2 cups water

2 turkey breast tenderloins (about 3/4 lb each)

1/2 teaspoon chili powder

1/2 teaspoon peppered seasoned salt

1. Heat oven to 350°F. Spray 11x7-inch (2-quart) glass baking dish with cooking spray. In 12-inch nonstick skillet, melt butter over medium-high heat. Cook onion and bell pepper in butter 2 to 3 minutes, stirring frequently, until tender. Stir in stuffing mix, corn and water. Spread stuffing mixture in baking dish.

2. Sprinkle both sides of turkey tenderloins with chili powder and peppered seasoned salt. Place on stuffing, pressing into stuffing mixture slightly. Spray sheet of foil with cooking spray. Cover baking dish with foil, sprayed side down.

3. Bake 1 hour. Uncover and bake 10 to 15 minutes longer or until juice of turkey is no longer pink when centers of thickest pieces are cut.

note from the nutritionist:

Add a little variety: For a refreshing accompaniment to this tasty casserole, toss a green salad with sliced jicama, onions, raspberries and a fruity vinaigrette dressing (or let them have reduced-fat ranch or Caesar dressing if they'd rather). Kids may need to try a new food several times before they decide they like it—hang in there.

1 Serving: Calories 330 (Calories from Fat 60); Total Fat 7g (Saturated Fat 2.5g); Cholesterol 85mg; Sodium 620mg; Total Carbohydrate 37g (Dietary Fiber 3g; Sugars 4g); Protein 31g

% Daily Value: Vitamin A 20%; Vitamin C 20%; Calcium 6%; Iron 20%

Exchanges: 2 1/2 Starch, 3 Very Lean Meat, 1 Fat

Carbohydrate Choices: 2 1/2

I like to run laps in gym—it makes me feel good.
Elizabeth H. age 8

Turkey and Corn Bread Casserole

Turkey and Stuffing Bake

Prep Time: 15 Minutes   **Start to Finish:** 55 Minutes

8 servings

3 cups chopped cooked turkey

1 bag (14 oz) frozen broccoli florets, thawed, drained

1 can (10 3/4 oz) condensed reduced-fat reduced-sodium cream of chicken soup

1/2 cup reduced-fat sour cream

1 1/2 cups shredded reduced-fat Swiss cheese (6 oz)

1 package (6 oz) stuffing mix for turkey

3/4 cup hot water

1. Heat oven to 350°F. In ungreased 13x9-inch (3-quart) glass baking dish, spread turkey. Top with broccoli.

2. In medium bowl, mix soup, sour cream and cheese; spread over broccoli. In large bowl, mix stuffing mix and hot water; sprinkle over soup mixture.

3. Bake uncovered 35 to 40 minutes or until hot and bubbly.

1 Serving: Calories 270 (Calories from Fat 80); Total Fat 9g (Saturated Fat 3.5g); Cholesterol 60mg; Sodium 990mg; Total Carbohydrate 23g (Dietary Fiber 2g; Sugars 3g); Protein 25g

% Daily Value: Vitamin A 20%; Vitamin C 15%; Calcium 20%; Iron 10%

Exchanges: 1 1/2 Starch, 3 Lean Meat

Carbohydrate Choices: 1 1/2

Wild Rice–Turkey Pot Pie

Prep Time: 10 Minutes   Start to Finish: 45 Minutes

6 servings

TURKEY FILLING

1 can (15 oz) cooked wild rice, drained

2 cups cubed cooked turkey (about 1 lb)

1 bag (1 lb) frozen mixed vegetables, thawed, drained

1 can (10 3/4 oz) condensed reduced-fat reduced-sodium cream of mushroom soup

1/4 cup fat-free (skim) milk

2 tablespoons instant minced onion

TOPPING

1 1/2 cups Original Bisquick® mix

3/4 cup fat-free (skim) milk

1 egg or 1/4 cup fat-free egg product

1. Heat oven to 400°F. Reserve 1/2 cup of the wild rice. In ungreased 2-quart casserole, stir remaining wild rice and remaining filling ingredients until mixed.

2. In medium bowl, stir reserved 1/2 cup wild rice and the topping ingredients with fork just until blended. Pour over turkey mixture.

3. Bake uncovered 25 to 35 minutes or until crust is golden brown.

note from DR. H:

It's a great idea to cook your own wild rice and use in place of the canned. In fact, planning and preparing as much as you can ahead of time will help you on your road to healthier eating—it's easier to make good choices when you aren't time-crunched.

> *Growing up in Colorado in the 1960s and '70s, we ate mostly meat and potatoes. I now know that it's best for my family to eat fresh fruit, vegetables and lean cuts of meat. I look for recipes that help me incorporate these ingredients and that taste good.*
>
> Alyson S.

1 Serving: Calories 370 (Calories from Fat 90); Total Fat 10g (Saturated Fat 2.5g); Cholesterol 75mg; Sodium 960mg; Total Carbohydrate 50g (Dietary Fiber 5g; Sugars 9g); Protein 23g

% Daily Value: Vitamin A 70%; Vitamin C 4%; Calcium 15%; Iron 15%

Exchanges: 2 1/2 Starch, 1/2 Other Carbohydrate, 1 Vegetable, 2 Lean Meat, 1/2 Fat

Carbohydrate Choices: 3

Impossibly Easy Turkey Taco Pie

Prep Time: 15 Minutes   Start to Finish: 50 Minutes

6 servings

1 lb ground turkey or lean (at least 80%) ground beef

1 medium onion, chopped (1/2 cup)

1 package (1.25 oz) taco seasoning mix

1 can (4.5 oz) chopped green chiles, drained

1/2 cup Original Bisquick® mix

1 cup fat-free (skim) milk

2 eggs or 1/2 cup fat-free egg product

1 medium tomato, chopped (3/4 cup)

1/2 cup shredded reduced-fat Monterey Jack cheese (2 oz)

1. Heat oven to 400°F. Spray 9-inch glass pie plate with cooking spray. In 10-inch skillet, cook turkey and onion over medium-high heat, stirring occasionally, until turkey is no longer pink; drain. Stir in taco seasoning mix. Spread in pie plate. Sprinkle with chiles.

2. In medium bowl, stir Bisquick mix, milk and eggs until blended. Pour into pie plate.

3. Bake 25 minutes. Top with tomato and cheese. Bake 8 to 10 minutes longer or until knife inserted in center comes out clean. Cool 5 minutes.

1 Serving: Calories 240 (Calories from Fat 90); Total Fat 10g (Saturated Fat 3.5g); Cholesterol 130mg; Sodium 870mg; Total Carbohydrate 15g (Dietary Fiber 2g; Sugars 7g); Protein 24g

% Daily Value: Vitamin A 25%; Vitamin C 8%; Calcium 20%; Iron 10%

Exchanges: 1/2 Starch, 1/2 Other Carbohydrate, 3 Lean Meat

Carbohydrate Choices: 1

My brother and I run after each other and play hug-tag. We get a lot of exercise that way.
Ruby O. age 9

Sizing Up Servings

One of the most important factors in energy balance is choosing healthy foods. Making smart selections, like whole grains, fruits, vegetables and lean meats, can help you cut calories. In addition to watching *what* you eat, pay attention to *how much* you eat. You probably don't pour your cereal into a measuring cup or weigh your apple at lunch. So how do you judge a serving size? Use these simple "by sight" ways to keep a watchful eye on your helpings:

1 medium fruit or vegetable = size of a tennis ball

1 cup = about the size of a woman's fist

1 ounce cheese = 2 dominoes or the size of a computer disk

1 teaspoon butter or peanut butter = about the size of the top of your thumb

1 ounce nuts = fits into palm of your hand

3 ounces meat, fish or poultry = deck of cards or an audiotape cassette

1 small banana = size of an eyeglass case

1 pancake or waffle serving = compact disc

1 serving of baked potato = computer mouse

1/2-cup serving of cooked rice, pasta, cereal, chips or pretzels = a rounded handful

To help control portions:

Split a meal at a restaurant, or take half of it home for the next day; many entrées are enough to feed two people.

Pour individual servings of snacks into bowls instead of eating right out of the bag or package.

Cook at home. It's easier to control portion sizes when you're in charge of making the meal.

Serve correct portion sizes before bringing dinner plates to the table to avoid overly large helpings and the temptation for seconds.

Read labels. Nutrition labels contain important information about nutrients and serving sizes.

Use smaller plates to keep your meal from looking skimpy.

Begin a couple of meals per week with an apple or a cup of soup to curb your appetite.

Nacho Chicken Casserole

Prep Time: 15 Minutes   **Start to Finish:** 1 Hour 15 Minutes

5 servings

2 cups diced cooked chicken

1/2 cup uncooked instant rice

1 can (14.5 oz) diced tomatoes, drained

1 can (10 3/4 oz) condensed reduced-fat reduced-sodium cream of chicken soup

1 can (11 oz) whole-kernel corn with red and green peppers, undrained

1 teaspoon taco seasoning mix (from 1.25-oz package)

1 1/2 cups shredded reduced-fat Cheddar cheese (6 oz)

1 cup tortilla chips

1. Heat oven to 350°F. Spray 2-quart casserole with cooking spray. In casserole, stir chicken, rice, tomatoes, soup, corn, taco seasoning mix and 1 cup of the cheese until well mixed.

2. Cover and bake about 1 hour or until rice is tender and mixture is heated through. Top with tortilla chips; sprinkle with remaining 1/2 cup cheese. Bake about 10 minutes longer or until filling is bubbly and cheese is melted.

1 Serving: Calories 350 (Calories from Fat 110); Total Fat 13g (Saturated Fat 4g); Cholesterol 55mg; Sodium 790mg; Total Carbohydrate 33g (Dietary Fiber 2g; Sugars 4g); Protein 28g

% Daily Value: Vitamin A 15%; Vitamin C 15%; Calcium 30%; Iron 15%

Exchanges: 2 Starch, 3 Lean Meat, 1/2 Fat

Carbohydrate Choices: 2

Nacho Chicken Casserole

Creamy Chicken and Ham over Rice

Prep Time: 10 Minutes   Start to Finish: 1 Hour 10 Minutes

5 servings

note from the nutritionist:

To add extra fiber, serve this delicious dish over converted brown or instant brown rice. If you can't find chicken tenders, cut 1 lb of boneless skinless chicken breasts halves lengthwise into strips.

1 can (10 3/4 oz) condensed reduced-fat reduced-sodium cream of chicken soup

1/2 cup reduced-fat sour cream

1 lb chicken breast tenders (not breaded)

1 package (2.5 oz) thinly sliced smoked ham, coarsely chopped

1 cup uncooked converted white rice

1 teaspoon parsley flakes

1. Heat oven to 325°F. Spray 11x7-inch (2-quart) glass baking dish with cooking spray. In small bowl, mix soup and sour cream. Arrange chicken in single layer in baking dish. Top with ham. Spoon soup mixture evenly over the top.

2. Bake uncovered about 1 hour or until chicken is no longer pink in center. Meanwhile, cook rice as directed on package for 4 servings. Sprinkle parsley over chicken mixture. Serve over rice.

1 Serving: Calories 380 (Calories from Fat 80); Total Fat 8g (Saturated Fat 3.5g); Cholesterol 75mg; Sodium 730mg; Total Carbohydrate 46g (Dietary Fiber 0g; Sugars 4g); Protein 30g

% Daily Value: Vitamin A 6%; Vitamin C 0%; Calcium 6%; Iron 15%

Exchanges: 3 Starch, 3 Very Lean Meat, 1 Fat

Carbohydrate Choices: 3

Grilled Paprika Chicken Dinner Packets

Prep Time: 20 Minutes   Start to Finish: 1 Hour

4 servings

4 boneless skinless chicken breast halves (about 1 1/4 lb)

2 cups cubed small red potatoes (4 or 5 potatoes)

1 1/2 cups baby-cut carrots, cut lengthwise in half

1 cup frozen cut green beans (from 1-lb bag)

1 cup chicken gravy (from 12-oz jar)

2 tablespoons all-purpose flour

1 teaspoon paprika

1/2 teaspoon dried thyme leaves

2 tablespoons finely chopped fresh parsley

1. Heat coals or gas grill for direct heat. Cut four 18x12-inch pieces of heavy-duty foil. Place chicken breast on each piece of foil. Top with potatoes, carrots and frozen green beans. In small bowl, mix gravy and flour until well blended; drizzle over chicken mixture. Sprinkle with paprika and thyme.

2. Fold foil over chicken and vegetables so edges meet. Seal edges, making tight 1/2-inch fold; fold again. Allow space on sides for circulation and expansion.

3. Cover and grill packets over medium heat 30 to 40 minutes, rotating packets 1/2 turn after 15 minutes, until juice of chicken is no longer pink when centers of thickest pieces are cut and vegetables are tender. Place packets on plates. Cut large X across top of each packet; fold back foil. Sprinkle with parsley.

note from DR. H:

Take any opportunity to add a little fun to dinnertime! These easy Chicken Dinner Packets just cry out for an outdoor (or even indoor) picnic. Have the kids help you get ready. Don't forget to end your picnic with a game of badminton, volleyball or other game. In the house? Try 25 jumping jacks or dancing.

Don't eat unhealthy foods all the time like cake, chips and candy.

Clarke S. age 9

1 Serving: Calories 310 (Calories from Fat 70); Total Fat 8g (Saturated Fat 2g); Cholesterol 85mg; Sodium 450mg; Total Carbohydrate 26g (Dietary Fiber 5g; Sugars 4g); Protein 35g

% Daily Value: Vitamin A 180%; Vitamin C 15%; Calcium 8%; Iron 20%

Exchanges: 1 1/2 Starch, 1 Vegetable, 4 Very Lean Meat, 1 Fat

Carbohydrate Choices: 1 1/2

Tomato-Basil
Chicken Casserole

Prep Time: 25 Minutes   **Start to Finish:** 1 Hour 15 Minutes

6 servings

note from DR. H:

Encourage your kids to share their creativity by helping you in the kitchen. Kids feel proud when they make something everyone likes— it helps build their self-esteem and confidence. They are learning a life skill, understanding the benefits of good nutrition and its relationship to good health.

2 cups uncooked gemelli pasta (8 oz)

2 cups diced cooked chicken

1 jar (26 oz) tomato pasta sauce (any hearty or thick variety)

1 medium zucchini, cut lengthwise in half, then cut into slices (1 1/2 cups)

1 can (3.8 oz) sliced ripe olives, drained

1 teaspoon dried basil leaves

1/4 cup shredded fresh Parmesan cheese

1. Heat oven to 375°F. Spray 2-quart casserole with cooking spray. Cook pasta as directed on package— except omit salt; drain.

2. In casserole, mix pasta and remaining ingredients except cheese.

3. Cover and bake 30 minutes. Sprinkle with cheese. Bake uncovered 15 to 20 minutes longer or until bubbly and thoroughly heated.

1 Serving: Calories 330 (Calories from Fat 90); Total Fat 10g (Saturated Fat 3g); Cholesterol 45mg; Sodium 1000mg; Total Carbohydrate 41g (Dietary Fiber 5g; Sugars 6g); Protein 21g

% Daily Value: Vitamin A 25%; Vitamin C 15%; Calcium 10%; Iron 20%

Exchanges: 2 1/2 Starch, 2 Lean Meat, 1/2 Fat

Carbohydrate Choices: 2 1/2

Sage Chicken and Potatoes

Prep Time: 15 Minutes   Start to Finish: 1 Hour 15 Minutes

4 servings

4 boneless skinless chicken breasts (about 1 lb)

3 medium unpeeled russet potatoes, cut into 3/4-inch pieces (3 cups)

1 1/2 cups baby-cut carrots

1 jar (12 oz) home-style chicken gravy

2 tablespoons Worcestershire sauce

1 teaspoon dried sage leaves

1/2 teaspoon garlic-pepper seasoning

1. Heat oven to 400°F. Spray 13x9-inch (3-quart) glass baking dish with cooking spray. Arrange chicken, potatoes and carrots in baking dish.

2. In small bowl, mix gravy, Worcestershire sauce, sage and garlic-pepper seasoning; pour over chicken and vegetables. Spray sheet of foil with cooking spray. Cover baking dish with foil, sprayed side down.

3. Bake 50 to 60 minutes or until vegetables are tender and juice of chicken is no longer pink when centers of thickest pieces are cut.

Another way to step into it is to think about how much time it will take to reach your daily goal. I have to walk about 75 minutes to reach a 10,000-step goal.

Greg S.

note from the nutritionist:

This recipe is a great source of iron—your body absorbs the iron from animal sources better and more efficiently than from plant sources. Vitamin C helps iron be better absorbed, so serve with tomato slices or an orange to get maximum efficiency.

1 Serving: Calories 310 (Calories from Fat 80); Total Fat 9g (Saturated Fat 2.5g); Cholesterol 70mg; Sodium 700mg; Total Carbohydrate 31g (Dietary Fiber 4g; Sugars 5g); Protein 29g

% Daily Value: Vitamin A 170%; Vitamin C 15%; Calcium 8%; Iron 20%

Exchanges: 2 Starch, 3 Very Lean Meat, 1 Fat

Carbohydrate Choices: 2

Fiesta Chicken Lasagna

Prep Time: 15 Minutes   **Start to Finish:** 1 Hour 25 Minutes

note from the nutritionist:

To reduce the sodium, use leftover chicken breasts in this great recipe. Slice the chicken breasts into strips, then sprinkle with a dash of ground red pepper (cayenne) or hot salsa.

8 servings

3 1/2 cups thick-and-chunky salsa

9 uncooked lasagna noodles

1 package (9 oz) frozen cooked Southwest-seasoned chicken breast strips, thawed

1 can (15 oz) black beans, rinsed, drained

1/4 cup chopped fresh cilantro

2 cups shredded reduced-fat Monterey Jack cheese (8 oz)

1. Heat oven to 375°F. In ungreased 13x9-inch (3-quart) glass baking dish, spread 1/4 cup of the salsa. Layer with 3 noodles and one-third each of the chicken, beans, cilantro, salsa and cheese. Repeat layers twice with remaining noodles, chicken, beans, cilantro, salsa and cheese. Cover baking dish with foil.

2. Bake 40 minutes. Uncover and bake 15 to 20 minutes longer or until hot in center. Let stand 10 minutes before cutting.

1 Serving: Calories 300 (Calories from Fat 80); Total Fat 9g (Saturated Fat 4.5g); Cholesterol 40mg; Sodium 1020mg; Total Carbohydrate 37g (Dietary Fiber 6g; Sugars 5g); Protein 22g

% Daily Value: Vitamin A 20%; Vitamin C 10%; Calcium 25%; Iron 20%

Exchanges: 2 1/2 Starch, 2 Very Lean Meat, 1 Fat

Carbohydrate Choices: 2

I lift weights at the school gym a couple times a week. That helps me get stronger and more fit and I can eat more (but not too much more).

Christian O. age 17

Fiesta Chicken Lasagna

Barbecue Chicken and Bean Casserole

Prep Time: 15 Minutes **Start to Finish:** 1 Hour 15 Minutes

6 servings

note from the nutritionist:

Kids usually like beans. And beans are so good for you: they add high amounts of fiber, are low in fat and high in protein. Their mild flavor makes them perfect for soups, salads and white chili. So go ahead, serve beans often.

1 lb boneless skinless chicken thighs

1 can (16 oz) baked beans

1 can (16 to 19 oz) cannellini beans, rinsed, drained

1/4 cup barbecue sauce

1 1/2 cups frozen cut green beans (from 1-lb bag), thawed, drained

1 cup coarsely chopped carrots (about 2 medium)

1 can (1.75 oz) shoestring potatoes (1 cup)

1. Heat oven to 375°F. Spray 2-quart casserole with cooking spray. Cut each chicken thigh into 4 pieces. In casserole, mix chicken and remaining ingredients except shoestring potatoes.

2. Cover and bake 30 minutes, stirring once. Uncover casserole; stir well. Bake uncovered 25 to 30 minutes longer, topping with shoestring potatoes for last 10 minutes, until chicken is no longer pink in center.

1 Serving: Calories 360 (Calories from Fat 90); Total Fat 10g (Saturated Fat 3g); Cholesterol 50mg; Sodium 510mg; Total Carbohydrate 46g (Dietary Fiber 11g; Sugars 9g); Protein 28g

% Daily Value: Vitamin A 100%; Vitamin C 8%; Calcium 15%; Iron 40%

Exchanges: 2 1/2 Starch, 1 Vegetable, 2 1/2 Lean Meat, 1/2 Fat

Carbohydrate Choices: 2

Beef and Bean Tortilla Bake

Prep Time: 20 Minutes   Start to Finish: 50 Minutes

6 servings

1 lb extra-lean (at least 90%) ground beef

1 can (15 oz) black beans, rinsed, drained

1 can (15 to 16 oz) pinto beans, rinsed, drained

1 can (14.5 oz) no-salt-added stewed tomatoes, undrained

1 package (1.25 oz) 40%-less-sodium taco seasoning mix

2/3 cup water

3/4 cup shredded reduced-fat sharp Cheddar cheese (3 oz)

3 spinach-flavor flour tortillas (8 inch), cut in half, then cut crosswise into 1/2-inch-wide strips

1. Heat oven to 350°F. In 12-inch skillet, cook beef over medium heat 8 to 10 minutes, stirring occasionally, until brown; drain. Stir in black beans, pinto beans, tomatoes, taco seasoning mix and water. Cook 2 to 4 minutes, stirring occasionally, until heated through. Stir in 1/2 cup of the cheese.

2. In 8-inch square (2-quart) glass baking dish, spread 2 cups of the beef mixture. Top with half of the tortilla strips. Spoon half of the remaining beef mixture over tortilla strips. Add remaining tortilla strips; top with remaining beef mixture.

3. Bake uncovered about 30 minutes or until bubbly and heated through. Sprinkle with remaining 1/4 cup cheese. Bake about 5 minutes longer or until cheese is melted. Cut into squares.

note from the nutritionist:

This recipe packs a big nutrition punch. You can use any flavor of flour tortillas, but the green tortillas add a nice color contrast. Add your favorite taco toppings— lettuce, tomatoes, salsa—but go light on the sour cream and guacamole or use the nonfat versions.

1 Serving: Calories 380 (Calories from Fat 80); Total Fat 9g (Saturated Fat 3.5g); Cholesterol 50mg; Sodium 940mg; Total Carbohydrate 51g (Dietary Fiber 10g; Sugars 4g); Protein 31g

% Daily Value: Vitamin A 10%; Vitamin C 10%; Calcium 25%; Iron 35%

Exchanges: 3 1/2 Starch, 3 Lean Meat

Carbohydrate Choices: 3

Garlic Cube Steaks

Prep Time: 15 Minutes   **Start to Finish:** 45 Minutes

4 servings

1 egg or 1/4 cup fat-free egg product

2 large cloves garlic, finely chopped

15 fat-free saltine crackers, crushed (1/2 cup)

4 boneless beef cube steaks (about 1 lb)

1/4 teaspoon garlic-pepper seasoning

2 tablespoons canola or soybean oil

1 medium onion, sliced

3/4 cup beef broth

2 teaspoons cornstarch

2 tablespoons chopped fresh parsley

1. In shallow dish, mix egg and garlic. In another shallow dish, place cracker crumbs. Sprinkle both sides of beef steaks with salt and garlic-pepper seasoning. Dip both sides of each steak into egg product mixture, then coat with cracker crumbs.

2. In 12-inch nonstick skillet, heat 1 tablespoon of the oil over medium-high heat. Cook beef in oil about 2 minutes or until brown. Turn beef, adding some of the remaining 1 tablespoon oil under each steak. Cook about 2 minutes longer or until brown. Add onion. Reduce heat to low. Cover and cook about 30 minutes or until beef is tender. Remove beef from skillet; cover to keep warm.

3. Meanwhile, in small bowl, mix broth and cornstarch. Add broth mixture to skillet; heat to boiling, stirring constantly. Serve sauce over beef; sprinkle with parsley.

note from DR. H:

Decide on a time for weekly family meetings. Discuss your goals and commitment to being active and eating well. If they are included from the get-go, the kids can share their ideas, understand your action plan better and may be more committed to being a part of the plan.

1 Serving: Calories 310 (Calories from Fat 140); Total Fat 16g (Saturated Fat 3.5g); Cholesterol 65mg; Sodium 450mg; Total Carbohydrate 14g (Dietary Fiber 1g; Sugars 2g); Protein 29g

% Daily Value: Vitamin A 8%; Vitamin C 4%; Calcium 4%; Iron 20%

Exchanges: 1 Starch, 3 1/2 Lean Meat, 1 Fat

Carbohydrate Choices: 1

I'm a meat person. Steak. Hamburger. Bratwurst. Fried chicken. Fried fish. Sausage. Now I use lean cuts of meat like skinless chicken to reduce fat and 'alternative' bacon and sausages.

Greg S.

Mini Meat Loaves

Prep Time: 10 Minutes   **Start to Finish:** 30 Minutes

4 servings (2 loaves each)

1/2 cup ketchup

2 tablespoons packed brown sugar

1 lb extra-lean (at least 90%) ground beef

1/3 cup old-fashioned or quick-cooking oats

1/2 teaspoon salt

1/4 teaspoon pepper

1 small onion, finely chopped (1/4 cup)

1 egg or 1/4 cup fat-free egg product

1. Heat oven to 450°F. In small bowl, stir ketchup and brown sugar until mixed; reserve 3 tablespoons. In large bowl, stir remaining ingredients and remaining ketchup mixture until well mixed.

2. Spray 13x9-inch pan with cooking spray. Place beef mixture in pan; pat into 10x3-inch rectangle. Cut lengthwise down center and then crosswise to form 8 loaves. Separate loaves, using spatula, so no edges are touching. Brush loaves with reserved 3 tablespoons ketchup mixture.

3. Bake uncovered 15 to 20 minutes or until meat thermometer inserted in center of loaves reads 160°F.

note from the nutritionist:

This dynamite recipe is a great one to serve often. The secret to getting these loaves done in 30 minutes? Their petite size makes them bake much faster. And the kids will love having their individual loaves. Serve with Four-Cheese Mashed Potato Casserole (page 204) and Marinated Carrot Salad (page 210).

1 Serving: Calories 280 (Calories from Fat 100); Total Fat 11g (Saturated Fat 4g); Cholesterol 125mg; Sodium 720mg; Total Carbohydrate 20g (Dietary Fiber 1g; Sugars 15g); Protein 25g

% Daily Value: Vitamin A 10%; Vitamin C 4%; Calcium 4%; Iron 20%

Exchanges: 1 Other Carbohydrate, 3 1/2 Medium-Fat Meat

Carbohydrate Choices: 1

Barbecue Pork Chops

Prep Time: 10 Minutes   **Start to Finish:** 30 Minutes

6 servings

1 cup barbecue-flavored potato chips (about 1 oz)

1/2 cup Original Bisquick® mix

1 egg, beaten

2 tablespoons barbecue sauce

6 boneless pork loin chops, 1/2 inch thick (about 1 1/2 lb)

1 tablespoon canola or soybean oil

3/4 cup barbecue sauce

1. Place potato chips in 1-gallon resealable plastic food-storage bag; crush with rolling pin. Add Bisquick mix to chips; mix well.

2. In small shallow dish, mix egg and 2 tablespoons barbecue sauce. Dip pork chops into egg mixture, then shake in bag to coat with Bisquick mixture.

3. In 12-inch nonstick skillet, heat oil over medium-low heat. Cook pork chops in oil 15 to 18 minutes, turning once, until golden brown on outside and no longer pink in center. Serve with 3/4 cup barbecue sauce.

To Freeze and Bake: Coat pork chops as directed, but do not cook. Wrap each pork chop in heavy-duty foil. Freeze up to 2 months. Place in refrigerator 8 hours or overnight until thawed. Cook as directed.

1 Serving: Calories 320 (Calories from Fat 130); Total Fat 14g (Saturated Fat 4g); Cholesterol 105mg; Sodium 580mg; Total Carbohydrate 21g (Dietary Fiber 0g; Sugars 10g); Protein 26g

% Daily Value: Vitamin A 2%; Vitamin C 2%; Calcium 4%; Iron 8%

Exchanges: 1 Starch, 1/2 Other Carbohydrate, 3 1/2 Lean Meat, 1/2 Fat

Carbohydrate Choices: 1 1/2

Parking farther away from the store and taking the stairs instead of the elevator works. I used to think I'd save time by parking close and saving 'wear and tear' on my kids. Now I know that if I park far away, I'm gaining exercise and my kids don't care that they are walking more steps.

Alyson S.

Barbecue Pork Chops

Pork Fajita Wraps

Prep Time: 20 Minutes   Start to Finish: 35 Minutes

4 wraps

1/4 cup lime juice

1 1/2 teaspoons ground cumin

3/4 teaspoon salt

4 cloves garlic, finely chopped

1/2 lb pork tenderloin, cut into very thin slices

1 large onion, thinly sliced

3 medium bell peppers, thinly sliced

4 flour tortillas (8 inch)

1. In shallow glass or plastic dish, mix lime juice, cumin, salt and garlic. Stir in pork. Cover and refrigerate, stirring occasionally, at least 15 minutes but no longer than 24 hours.

2. Remove pork from marinade; reserve marinade. Heat 12-inch nonstick skillet over medium-high heat. Cook pork in skillet 3 minutes, stirring once. Stir in onion, bell peppers and marinade. Cook 5 to 8 minutes, stirring frequently, until onion and peppers are crisp-tender.

3. Place one-fourth of the pork mixture on center of each tortilla. Fold one end of tortilla up about 1 inch over pork mixture; fold right and left sides over folded end, overlapping.

note from the nutritionist:

One bell pepper packs a real nutritional punch. It contains one and one-half times the vitamin C your body needs daily. You can serve these flavorful fajitas with 1/2 cup reduced-fat sour cream or plain yogurt and 1/2 cup salsa stirred together.

1 Wrap: Calories 260 (Calories from Fat 50); Total Fat 6g (Saturated Fat 1.5g); Cholesterol 35mg; Sodium 680mg; Total Carbohydrate 35g (Dietary Fiber 3g; Sugars 4g); Protein 18g

% Daily Value: Vitamin A 8%; Vitamin C 70%; Calcium 8%; Iron 20%

Exchanges: 2 1/2 Starch, 1 1/2 Lean Meat

Carbohydrate Choices: 2

Pork Fajita Wraps

Cheesy Noodle Casserole (page 187)

6

KID-LOVIN' LUNCHES

Buffalo-Style Chicken Nuggets

Prep Time: 10 Minutes   Start to Finish: 25 Minutes

4 servings

1 1/2 cups Corn Chex® cereal

1/2 cup Original Bisquick® mix

2 teaspoons paprika

1/4 teaspoon seasoned salt

1/4 teaspoon ground red pepper (cayenne)

1 tablespoon canola or soybean oil

1 teaspoon red pepper sauce

1 lb boneless skinless chicken breasts, cut into 2-inch pieces

1/4 cup fat-free sour cream

1/4 cup reduced-fat ranch dressing

1. Heat oven to 425°F. Place cereal in 1-gallon resealable plastic food-storage bag; crush with rolling pin. Add Bisquick mix, paprika, seasoned salt and red pepper to cereal; mix well.

2. In small bowl, mix oil and red pepper sauce. Coat chicken pieces with oil mixture.

3. Shake about 6 chicken pieces at a time in bag of cereal mixture until coated. Shake off any extra mixture. On ungreased cookie sheet, place chicken pieces in single layer.

4. Bake about 10 minutes or until chicken is no longer pink in center. Meanwhile, in small bowl, mix sour cream and dressing. Serve sauce with chicken.

note from the nutritionist:

Add some wholesome veggies to accompany your lunch. Try a side of crunchy dippers such as celery and carrot sticks, green bell pepper strips and cucumber chips to serve with these spicy nuggets and zippy sauce. Dip in your favorite reduced-fat or fat-free dressing.

1 Serving: Calories 310 (Calories from Fat 110); Total Fat 12g (Saturated Fat 2g); Cholesterol 75mg; Sodium 640mg; Total Carbohydrate 24g (Dietary Fiber 1g; Sugars 3g); Protein 28g

% Daily Value: Vitamin A 20%; Vitamin C 2%; Calcium 10%; Iron 30%

Exchanges: 1 1/2 Starch, 3 Very Lean Meat, 2 Fat

Carbohydrate Choices: 1 1/2

One easy way to reduce sugar is to use natural peanut butter (no added sugar) and an artificially sweetened jelly when making PBJ. My kids didn't notice the change at all, but it's about 70 calories we are able to lower.

Deb M.

Buffalo-Style Chicken Nuggets

Go for Grains and Fiber Every Day

Nutrition experts suggest you get most of your carbohydrates from the complex carbohydrates found in grains, vegetables and fruits. They also recommend 25 to 30 grams of fiber every day to stay healthy.

Whole Grains

Whole-grain foods are excellent sources of soluble fiber because they include all parts of the grain, as well as all the grain's nutrients. Choosing the "whole food" gives you the whole package of health benefits.

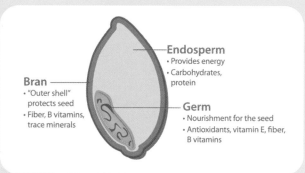

Endosperm
• Provides energy
• Carbohydrates, protein

Bran
• "Outer shell" protects seed
• Fiber, B vitamins, trace minerals

Germ
• Nourishment for the seed
• Antioxidants, vitamin E, fiber, B vitamins

Whole-Grain Boosters

Try to get at least three servings from whole grains every day. Boost your whole grains by choosing:

Whole-grain hot or cold cereals, like oatmeal or farina. Look for a whole-grain seal on the package.

Whole wheat, whole-grain or multigrain breads, bagels, English muffins, pita breads and tortillas.

Brown rice over white rice, hulled barley over pearled barley.

Whole wheat pasta over plain pasta. To get used to it, mix half whole wheat pasta and half plain.

Whole wheat flour for half the white flour called for when baking breads, bran or fruit muffins, pancakes, biscuits or waffles.

Less-common whole grains like whole-grain barley, bulgur, kasha and quinoa.

Fiber

You may have heard of the two types of fiber in foods. **Soluble fiber** dissolves and becomes gummy in water, slows digestion and promotes a sense of fullness. **Insoluble fiber**, known as roughage, speeds the passage of food through the intestines. You can boost your soluble and insoluble fiber amount by eating:

A variety of fresh fruits and vegetables, including the skins and seeds.

Fiber-rich foods like air-popped popcorn, nuts and soy nuts, raisins and other dried fruits.

High-fiber cereal with fruit for breakfast, a whole-grain-bread sandwich with veggies for lunch and vegetable soup with whole-grain crackers for dinner.

Fiber cereals, such as Fiber One®, or using bran when making muffins, breads or cookies.

Beans in chilis, soups, stews, casseroles, tortillas, tacos and other ethnic dishes.

Salads and soups topped with ground flax seed, popcorn, wheat germ or high-fiber cereal.

Pancakes, waffles or toast topped with fruit sauces with seeds, such as strawberries, raspberries or kiwifruit.

Chicken and Berry Salad

Prep Time: 15 Minutes **Start to Finish:** 15 Minutes

3 servings

5 cups bite-size pieces mixed salad greens

1 cup strawberry halves

1/2 cup blueberries

1/2 cup raspberries

1/4 cup honey-roasted peanuts

1/4 cup fat-free vinaigrette dressing

2 tablespoons crumbled blue cheese

1 package (6 oz) refrigerated grilled chicken breast strips, cut in half if necessary

In large bowl, toss all ingredients.

note from the nutritionist:

Check out this tasty salad—it's a very nutrient-dense recipe. That means that for the calories, there are many nutrients, like vitamins A and C, calcium and iron. If you prefer a fruitier flavor, you can use fat-free raspberry vinaigrette in place of regular vinaigrette.

1 Serving: Calories 250 (Calories from Fat 100); Total Fat 11g (Saturated Fat 2.5g); Cholesterol 50mg; Sodium 500mg; Total Carbohydrate 18g (Dietary Fiber 6g; Sugars 12g); Protein 24g

% Daily Value: Vitamin A 60%; Vitamin C 90%; Calcium 10%; Iron 15%

Exchanges: 1 Fruit, 3 1/2 Very Lean Meat, 2 Fat

Carbohydrate Choices: 1

Turkey Mac Skillet

Prep Time: 30 Minutes **Start to Finish:** 30 Minutes

6 servings

2 teaspoons canola or soybean oil

1 1/4 lb ground turkey breast

1 cup uncooked wagon wheel pasta (2 oz)

1/2 cup thick-and-chunky salsa

1 cup water

1/2 teaspoon salt

Dash of pepper

2 medium stalks celery, thinly sliced (1 cup)

1 medium tomato, chopped (3/4 cup)

2 cans (8 oz each) tomato sauce

1. In 12-inch skillet, heat oil over medium-high heat. Cook turkey in oil 5 to 7 minutes, stirring occasionally, until no longer pink; drain.

2. Stir in remaining ingredients. Heat to boiling; reduce heat to low. Cover and simmer 8 to 10 minutes or until pasta is tender.

1 Serving: Calories 260 (Calories from Fat 70); Total Fat 7g (Saturated Fat 1.5g); Cholesterol 65mg; Sodium 830mg; Total Carbohydrate 25g (Dietary Fiber 3g; Sugars 4g); Protein 25g

% Daily Value: Vitamin A 20%; Vitamin C 15%; Calcium 4%; Iron 15%

Exchanges: 1 1/2 Starch, 1 Vegetable, 2 1/2 Lean Meat

Carbohydrate Choices: 1 1/2

When we walk, we visit with people walking their dogs and with each other. It is great family time. The kids automatically tell me about their day and their worries. I really treasure this time, even though I wasn't looking forward to it at the beginning.

Deb M.

Cheeseburger Calzones

Prep Time: 20 Minutes   Start to Finish: 40 Minutes

5 calzones

1/2 lb lean (at least 80%) ground beef

3 tablespoons ketchup

1 teaspoon yellow mustard

1 teaspoon instant minced onion

2 cups Original Bisquick® mix

1/2 cup boiling water

1 cup shredded reduced-fat
Cheddar cheese (4 oz)

1 egg, beaten

1 teaspoon sesame seed

1. Heat oven to 375°F. In 10-inch skillet, cook beef over medium-high heat 6 to 8 minutes, stirring occasionally, until brown; drain. Stir in ketchup, mustard and onion.

2. In medium bowl, stir Bisquick mix and boiling water with fork until dough forms. Divide dough into 5 equal pieces. Place dough pieces on surface sprinkled with Bisquick mix; roll in Bisquick mix to coat. Press each piece into 6-inch round, about 1/4 inch thick.

3. Spoon one-fifth of the beef mixture onto one side of each dough round to within 1/2 inch of edges. Top beef on each round with cheese. Fold dough in half, covering filling. Press edges with tines of fork to seal. Place calzones on ungreased cookie sheet.

4. Brush calzones with egg. Sprinkle with sesame seed. Bake 15 to 20 minutes or until golden brown.

note from the nutritionist:

It's often hard to find a quick, yet good-for-you meal on the go. These calzones are perfect: simply wrap a baked calzone in foil to keep it warm while you're on the run.

Having my own step counter is great! Jumping rope really makes the steps go up fast.

Ruby O. age 9

1 Calzone: Calories 390 (Calories from Fat 190); Total Fat 21g (Saturated Fat 9g); Cholesterol 95mg; Sodium 970mg; Total Carbohydrate 32g (Dietary Fiber 0g; Sugars 7g); Protein 18g

% Daily Value: Vitamin A 8%; Vitamin C 0%; Calcium 20%; Iron 15%

Exchanges: 1 1/2 Starch, 1/2 Other Carbohydrate, 2 High-Fat Meat, 1 Fat

Carbohydrate Choices: 2

Beef and Cheese Foldover Sandwiches

Prep Time: 20 Minutes	Start to Finish: 45 Minutes

note from DR. H:

Make it fun—choose activities you enjoy and ask friends to join you. The more fun you have, the more likely you'll be able to stick to your plan.

5 sandwiches

2 cups Original Bisquick® mix

1/2 cup boiling water

1 tablespoon Dijon mustard

10 oz deli shaved cooked roast beef

1 cup shredded Swiss cheese (4 oz)

1 egg

1 tablespoon water

1. Heat oven to 375°F. Spray cookie sheet with cooking spray. In medium bowl, stir Bisquick mix and boiling water with fork until dough forms. If dough is dry, stir in additional 1 tablespoon water. Divide dough into 5 pieces. Place dough pieces on surface sprinkled with Bisquick mix; roll in Bisquick mix to coat. Press each piece into 6-inch square, about 1/8 inch thick.

2. Spread about 1/2 teaspoon of the mustard on each dough square to within 1/2 inch of edges. Arrange one-fifth of the beef on each square to within 1/2 inch of edges, folding to fit if needed. Top each with cheese. Fold each square diagonally in half (moisten edges with water if desired). Press edges with tines of fork to seal. Place on cookie sheet.

3. In small bowl, beat egg and water; brush over sandwiches. Bake 20 to 25 minutes or until crust is golden brown.

To Freeze and Bake: Place unbaked sandwiches without egg wash on ungreased cookie sheet. Freeze uncovered 2 to 3 hours or until solid; arrange in single layer in container to prevent breaking. Seal well and freeze up to 2 months. To bake, place on greased cookie sheet and brush with egg-water mixture. Bake at 350°F for 25 to 30 minutes or until crust is golden brown.

1 Sandwich: Calories 430 (Calories from Fat 200); Total Fat 23g (Saturated Fat 9g); Cholesterol 110mg; Sodium 860mg; Total Carbohydrate 30g (Dietary Fiber 0g; Sugars 4g); Protein 26g

% Daily Value: Vitamin A 6%; Vitamin C 0%; Calcium 30%; Iron 20%

Exchanges: 2 Starch, 3 Lean Meat, 2 1/2 Fat

Carbohydrate Choices: 2

I made this recipe all by myself, and it was great. I like to help make lunch and dinner with my family. We try to eat dinner together whenever we can.

Carlon O. age 14

Beef and Cheese Foldover Sandwiches

Ranch Cheeseburgers

Prep Time: 20 Minutes   Start to Finish: 20 Minutes

4 sandwiches

1 lb lean (at least 80%) ground beef

1/4 cup finely chopped onion

1/4 cup chopped fresh parsley

1/4 cup fat-free ranch dressing

1/4 teaspoon coarsely ground pepper

4 slices (about 3/4 oz each) reduced-fat Cheddar or American cheese

4 whole-grain sandwich buns, split

12 dill pickle slices

1. Heat closed medium-size contact grill for 5 minutes. In medium bowl, mix beef, onion, parsley, 3 tablespoons of the dressing and the pepper. Shape mixture into 4 patties, about 3/4 inch thick.

2. Place patties on grill. Close grill. Grill 4 to 6 minutes or until meat thermometer inserted in center of patties reads 160°F and patties are no longer pink in center. Top each patty with cheese slice. Let stand on grill about 3 minutes or until cheese is melted.

3. Spread remaining ranch dressing on cut sides of buns. Place cheese-topped patties and pickles in buns.

1 Sandwich: Calories 340 (Calories from Fat 140); Total Fat 16g (Saturated Fat 6g); Cholesterol 75mg; Sodium 830mg; Total Carbohydrate 23g (Dietary Fiber 3g; Sugars 6g); Protein 29g

% Daily Value: Vitamin A 15%; Vitamin C 6%; Calcium 20%; Iron 20%

Exchanges: 1 1/2 Starch, 3 1/2 Lean Meat, 1 Fat

Carbohydrate Choices: 1 1/2

I like shooting baskets when friends come over. My dad shoots baskets with me, too.

Carlon O. age 14

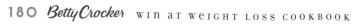

Chicken and Veggie Pizza

Prep Time: 10 Minutes   **Start to Finish:** 35 Minutes

8 servings

2 cups Original Bisquick® mix

1/3 cup very hot water

3/4 cup spinach dip

1 cup chopped cooked chicken

1 medium tomato, seeded, chopped (3/4 cup)

1 package (8 oz) sliced fresh mushrooms (3 cups)

1 1/2 cups shredded part-skim mozzarella cheese (6 oz)

1. Move oven rack to lowest position. Heat oven to 450°F. Spray 12-inch pizza pan with cooking spray.

2. In medium bowl, stir Bisquick mix, hot water and 1/4 cup of the spinach dip with fork until soft dough forms; beat vigorously 20 strokes. Press dough in pizza pan, using fingers dipped in Bisquick mix; pinch edge to form 1/2-inch rim. Bake 7 minutes.

3. Spread remaining 1/2 cup spinach dip over partially baked crust. Sprinkle with chicken, tomato and mushrooms. Sprinkle with cheese.

4. Bake 12 to 15 minutes or until crust is brown and cheese is melted.

We like having little celebrations—it gives us something to look forward to. We just use flavored sparkling water or sparkling apple or pear juice in special glasses.

Steve O.

1 Serving: Calories 270 (Calories from Fat 130); Total Fat 15g (Saturated Fat 5g); Cholesterol 30mg; Sodium 680mg; Total Carbohydrate 23g (Dietary Fiber 1g; Sugars 4g); Protein 14g

% Daily Value: Vitamin A 15%; Vitamin C 4%; Calcium 25%; Iron 10%

Exchanges: 1 1/2 Starch, 1 1/2 Lean Meat, 2 Fat

Carbohydrate Choices: 1 1/2

Stuffed-Crust Pizza

Prep Time: 20 Minutes   Start to Finish: 35 Minutes

8 servings

3 cups Original Bisquick® mix

2/3 cup very hot water

2 tablespoons olive or canola oil

4 sticks mozzarella or Colby-Monterey Jack cheese (from 10-oz package), cut lengthwise in half

1 can (8 oz) pizza sauce

1 cup shredded Italian cheese blend (4 oz)

1 cup sliced fresh mushrooms (3 oz)

1 small green bell pepper, chopped (1/2 cup)

1 can (2.25 oz) sliced ripe olives, drained

1. Move oven rack to lowest position. Heat oven to 450°F. Spray 12-inch pizza pan with cooking spray.

2. In large bowl, stir Bisquick mix, hot water and oil with fork until soft dough forms; beat vigorously 20 strokes. If dough is dry, stir in additional 1 tablespoon water. Cover and let stand 8 minutes.

3. Pat or press dough in bottom and 1 inch over side of pizza pan. Place sticks of cheese along edge of dough, overlapping if necessary. Fold 1-inch edge of dough over and around cheese; press to seal. Bake 7 minutes.

4. Spread pizza sauce over partially baked crust. Sprinkle with 1/2 cup of the Italian cheese, the mushrooms, bell pepper and olives. Sprinkle with remaining 1/2 cup cheese.

5. Bake 9 to 12 minutes or until crust is golden brown and cheese is melted.

1 Serving: Calories 320 (Calories from Fat 150); Total Fat 17g (Saturated Fat 6g); Cholesterol 20mg; Sodium 1050mg; Total Carbohydrate 32g (Dietary Fiber 1g; Sugars 5g); Protein 11g

% Daily Value: Vitamin A 10%; Vitamin C 10%; Calcium 30%; Iron 10%

Exchanges: 2 Starch, 1 High-Fat Meat, 1 1/2 Fat

Carbohydrate Choices: 2

I like to drink water—my parents pack water for me every day in my lunch box.
Elizabeth H. age 8

Stuffed-Crust Pizza

Canadian Bacon Pizza with Cheddar-Mustard Sauce

Prep Time: 25 Minutes   Start to Finish: 1 Hour

8 servings

CRUST

8 cups frozen shredded hash brown potatoes, thawed, drained

2 tablespoons butter or margarine, melted

2 eggs, beaten, or 1/2 cup fat-free egg product

1/2 cup all-purpose flour

1/2 teaspoon salt

CHEDDAR-MUSTARD SAUCE

4 oz pasteurized prepared cheese product loaf, cut into 1-inch cubes

2 tablespoons fat-free (skim) milk

1 teaspoon grated Parmesan cheese

1/2 teaspoon Dijon mustard

TOPPING

1 package (3.5 oz) pizza-style sliced Canadian-style bacon

6 eggs or 1 1/2 cups fat-free egg product

1/4 cup fat-free (skim) milk

1/4 teaspoon salt

1/8 teaspoon pepper

1 tablespoon butter or margarine

1 tablespoon chopped fresh chives

1. Heat oven to 425°F. Spray 12-inch pizza pan with cooking spray or grease with shortening. In large bowl, toss potatoes, 1/4 cup melted butter, 2 eggs, the flour and 1/2 teaspoon salt. Press potato mixture in pan. Bake 20 to 25 minutes or until edges are golden brown.

2. Meanwhile, in small microwavable bowl, cover and microwave cheese product cubes and 2 tablespoons milk on High 1 minute; stir until smooth. Stir in Parmesan cheese and mustard until well blended. Spread 1/2 cup of the cheese sauce over potato crust; top with Canadian bacon. Cover remaining sauce to keep warm.

3. Bake 5 to 7 minutes longer or until Canadian bacon is heated through.

4. Meanwhile, in medium bowl, beat 6 eggs, 1/4 cup milk, 1/4 teaspoon salt and the pepper with fork or wire whisk until well mixed.

5. In a 10-inch skillet, heat 1 tablespoon butter over medium heat just until butter begins to sizzle. Pour egg mixture into skillet. As mixture begins to set at bottom and side, gently lift cooked portions with spatula so that thin, uncooked portion can flow to bottom. Avoid constant stirring. Cook 3 to 4 minutes or until eggs are thickened throughout but still moist.

6. Spoon scrambled eggs over hot crust. Drizzle with remaining 1/2 cup cheese sauce. Sprinkle with chives. Use a spatula to lift servings from pan.

Tortellini Minestrone Casserole

Prep Time: 15 Minutes   Start to Finish: 1 Hour 15 Minutes

4 servings

1 package (9 oz) refrigerated three-cheese tortellini

1 1/2 cups frozen mixed vegetables (from 1-lb bag)

1 can (14.5 oz) diced tomatoes with basil, garlic and oregano, undrained

1 can (15 to 16 oz) great northern beans, rinsed, drained

1 can (8 oz) tomato sauce

1/2 cup water

1/4 cup shredded fresh Parmesan cheese (1 oz)

1. Heat oven to 375°F. In ungreased 8-inch square (2-quart) glass baking dish, mix all ingredients except cheese. Cover baking dish with foil.

2. Bake 45 minutes. Uncover and stir well. Sprinkle with cheese. Bake uncovered 10 to 15 minutes longer or until bubbly and cheese is melted.

note from the nutritionist:

Change up the mix by trying colorful pinto or red kidney beans in this great-tasting recipe. Cannellini beans make a good substitute for the great northern beans, too.

What are healthy foods? Broccoli, and cantaloupe, and strawberries, and corn, and peas.

North S. age 5

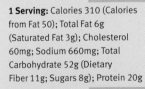

1 Serving: Calories 310 (Calories from Fat 50); Total Fat 6g (Saturated Fat 3g); Cholesterol 60mg; Sodium 660mg; Total Carbohydrate 52g (Dietary Fiber 11g; Sugars 8g); Protein 20g

% Daily Value: Vitamin A 80%; Vitamin C 20%; Calcium 25%; Iron 30%

Exchanges: 2 1/2 Starch, 1/2 Other Carbohydrate, 1 Vegetable, 1 1/2 Very Lean Meat, 1/2 Fat

Carbohydrate Choices: 3

Triple-Cheese Ravioli

Prep Time: 15 Minutes   **Start to Finish:** 40 Minutes

4 servings

note from the nutritionist:

Come and eat! Serve with a crisp green salad drizzled with balsamic vinegar and olive oil, along with Cheesy Italian Tomato Toasts (page 76).

1 package (9 oz) refrigerated cheese-filled ravioli

2 large tomatoes, chopped (2 cups)

1 small onion, chopped (1/4 cup)

1/2 cup sliced fresh mushrooms (1 1/2 oz)

1/4 cup dry red wine or chicken broth

1 tablespoon chopped fresh or 1 teaspoon dried basil leaves

1/8 teaspoon salt

1/8 teaspoon pepper

1 clove garlic, finely chopped

1/2 cup ricotta cheese

2 tablespoons grated Parmesan cheese

1. Heat oven to 325°F. Cook and drain ravioli as directed on package.

2. Meanwhile, in 10-inch skillet, cook remaining ingredients except cheeses over medium-high heat about 5 minutes, stirring frequently, until tomatoes are soft.

3. In ungreased 8-inch square (2-quart) glass baking dish, spread ravioli. Spread ricotta cheese over ravioli. Pour tomato mixture over top. Sprinkle with Parmesan cheese. Bake uncovered 20 to 25 minutes or until hot in center.

1 Serving: Calories 190 (Calories from Fat 70); Total Fat 8g (Saturated Fat 4.5g); Cholesterol 75mg; Sodium 480mg; Total Carbohydrate 18g (Dietary Fiber 2g; Sugars 3g); Protein 13g

% Daily Value: Vitamin A 20%; Vitamin C 15%; Calcium 25%; Iron 8%

Exchanges: 1 Starch, 1 1/2 Medium-Fat Meat

Carbohydrate Choices: 1

Cheesy Noodle Casserole

Prep Time: 20 Minutes   Start to Finish: 55 Minutes

6 servings

4 cups uncooked wide egg noodles
(8 oz)

3 cups frozen broccoli florets (from
14-oz bag)

1/2 cup fat-free (skim) milk

1/2 cup fat-free sour cream

1 package (8 oz) shredded American
and Cheddar cheese blend (2 cups)

1/4 teaspoon pepper

3/4 cup reduced-fat bite-size square
cheese crackers, finely crushed
(1/2 cup crushed)

1. Heat oven to 375°F. Spray 2-quart casserole with cooking spray. Cook noodles as directed on package, adding broccoli for last 2 minutes of cooking time. Drain noodles and broccoli in colander.

2. In same saucepan (not over heat), stir milk and sour cream until smooth. Stir in cheese and pepper. Stir in noodles and broccoli. Spoon into casserole. Sprinkle with crushed crackers.

3. Bake uncovered 25 to 35 minutes or until bubbly and top is golden brown.

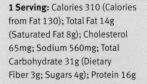

note from the nutritionist:

This kid-friendly casserole is great with sliced apples or applesauce or a salad of sliced fresh tomatoes drizzled with vinaigrette dressing.

1 Serving: Calories 310 (Calories from Fat 130); Total Fat 14g (Saturated Fat 8g); Cholesterol 65mg; Sodium 560mg; Total Carbohydrate 31g (Dietary Fiber 3g; Sugars 4g); Protein 16g

% Daily Value: Vitamin A 35%; Vitamin C 25%; Calcium 25%; Iron 10%

Exchanges: 1 1/2 Starch, 1 Vegetable, 1 1/2 High-Fat Meat, 1/2 Fat

Carbohydrate Choices: 2

Parmesan Rice and Peas with Bacon

Prep Time: 10 Minutes   **Start to Finish:** 45 Minutes

8 servings

2 slices bacon, chopped

1 medium onion, chopped (1/2 cup)

1 cup uncooked long-grain regular rice

1 can (14 oz) chicken broth

1/2 cup water

1 cup frozen baby sweet peas (from 1-lb bag), thawed

3/4 cup grated Parmesan cheese

1/8 teaspoon pepper

1. In 2-quart saucepan, cook bacon over medium heat 3 to 4 minutes, stirring occasionally, until crisp. Stir in onion. Cook about 1 minute, stirring occasionally, until onion is tender.

2. Stir in rice until well coated with bacon drippings. Stir in broth and water. Heat to boiling; reduce heat to low. Cover and simmer about 20 minutes or until rice is tender and broth is absorbed.

3. Gently stir in peas. Cover and cook 1 to 2 minutes or until peas are hot; remove from heat. Stir in cheese and pepper.

1 Serving: Calories 160 (Calories from Fat 40); Total Fat 4.5g (Saturated Fat 2g); Cholesterol 10mg; Sodium 430mg; Total Carbohydrate 24g (Dietary Fiber 1g; Sugars 2g); Protein 8g

% Daily Value: Vitamin A 4%; Vitamin C 0%; Calcium 15%; Iron 8%

Exchanges: 1 1/2 Starch, 1/2 High-Fat Meat

Carbohydrate Choices: 1 1/2

It's tempting in the winter to just stay inside, but we get the kids out to play in the snow. They like building snow forts, skating, sledding, tubing, cross country skiing.

Steve O.

Parmesan Rice and Peas with Bacon

Caesar Shrimp Salad

Prep Time: 25 Minutes   **Start to Finish:** 25 Minutes

8 servings

4 cups uncooked medium pasta shells (10 oz)

1 cup shredded Parmesan cheese (4 oz)

1 cup reduced-fat creamy Caesar dressing

8 medium green onions, sliced (1/2 cup)

1 package (24 oz) frozen cooked peeled deveined shrimp, thawed, drained and tails peeled

1 bag (10 oz) bite-size pieces romaine lettuce (7 cups)

2 cups Caesar-flavored croutons

1. Cook pasta as directed on package—except omit salt; drain. Rinse with cold water; drain.

2. In very large (4-quart) bowl, toss pasta, cheese, dressing, onions and shrimp. Just before serving, add lettuce and croutons; toss.

1 Serving: Calories 460 (Calories from Fat 80); Total Fat 9g (Saturated Fat 3.5g); Cholesterol 175mg; Sodium 870mg; Total Carbohydrate 64g (Dietary Fiber 5g; Sugars 6g); Protein 33g

% Daily Value: Vitamin A 30%; Vitamin C 25%; Calcium 25%; Iron 35%

Exchanges: 4 Starch, 3 Very Lean Meat, 1 Fat

Carbohydrate Choices: 4

It goes faster if I mix jogging with walking. If I don't set aside time for two meaningful walks a day, I can't even come close to my stepping goal.

Greg S.

Turkey, Rice and Romaine Salad

Prep Time: 45 Minutes   Start to Finish: 1 Hour

10 servings

SALAD

3 cups uncooked instant brown rice

2 tablespoons lemon juice

1/2 lb smoked turkey breast, cut into
1x1/4x1/4-inch strips (2 cups)

1 large red bell pepper, cut into
2x1/4-inch strips

8 medium green onions, sliced
(1/2 cup)

1 1/2 cups thin jicama strips
(about 2 inches long)

10 cups bite-size pieces
romaine lettuce

RICE VINEGAR DRESSING

2/3 cup rice vinegar

1/3 cup canola or soybean oil

1 tablespoon sugar

2 tablespoons Dijon mustard

1/2 teaspoon salt

1/2 teaspoon pepper

1. Cook rice as directed on package, omitting margarine and salt. In very large (4-quart) bowl, toss rice and lemon juice. In 15x10x1-inch pan, spread rice. Place in freezer 15 minutes or in refrigerator 1 hour to chill.

2. When rice is cold, return to large bowl. Stir in remaining salad ingredients.

3. In small bowl, beat all dressing ingredients with wire whisk until blended. Pour over rice mixture; toss lightly to coat.

note from DR. H:

Expect protest: At first, your kids may reject your ideas of snacking on fruits and vegetables. The latest research shows, however, that kids are more likely to eventually accept them at home than when they're served at school or in other settings. So don't give up—you are giving your kids the gift of good health and good nutrition.

1 Serving: Calories 250 (Calories from Fat 80); Total Fat 9g (Saturated Fat 0.5g); Cholesterol 10mg; Sodium 480mg; Total Carbohydrate 35g (Dietary Fiber 5g; Sugars 5g); Protein 8g

% Daily Value: Vitamin A 45%; Vitamin C 80%; Calcium 4%; Iron 8%

Exchanges: 2 Starch, 1/2 Lean Meat, 1 1/2 Fat

Carbohydrate Choices: 2

SIDE SALADS AND VEGETABLES

7

Dilled Cucumber-Tomato Salad

Prep Time: 15 Minutes   **Start to Finish:** 15 Minutes

5 servings (1/2 cup each)

1/4 cup plain fat-free yogurt

1 small clove garlic, finely chopped

1/2 teaspoon dried dill weed

1/4 teaspoon sugar

1/8 teaspoon salt

3 large plum (Roma) tomatoes, seeded, diced (1 1/2 cups)

1 medium cucumber, peeled, seeded and cubed (1 cup)

1. In medium bowl, mix yogurt, garlic, dill weed, sugar and salt.

2. Fold in tomatoes and cucumber. Serve immediately.

note from the nutritionist:

Serving vegetable salads is a great way to make a dent in your recommended three to five servings of vegetables daily. If you use an English or seedless cucumber instead of a regular cucumber, you won't have to peel or seed it.

1 Serving: Calories 25 (Calories from Fat 0); Total Fat 0g (Saturated Fat 0g); Cholesterol 0mg; Sodium 75mg; Total Carbohydrate 5g (Dietary Fiber 0g; Sugars 2g); Protein 1g

% Daily Value: Vitamin A 8%; Vitamin C 20%; Calcium 4%; Iron 2%

Exchanges: Free

Carbohydrate Choices: 0

I grew up in a relatively poor household where fresh fruits and vegetables were considered a luxury. As an adult, I know that they are so important for my family that it doesn't matter what they cost—we have them every day.

Alyson S.

Dilled Cucumber-Tomato Salad

Easy Bean Salad

Prep Time: 20 Minutes   Start to Finish: 1 Hour 20 Minutes

14 servings (1/2 cup each)

1 can (15 to 16 oz) great northern beans, rinsed, drained

1 can (15 to 16 oz) kidney beans, rinsed, drained

1 can (15 to 16 oz) garbanzo beans, rinsed, drained

1 large cucumber, chopped (1 1/2 cups)

1 large tomato, chopped (1 cup)

1/2 medium red onion, chopped (1 cup)

3 tablespoons basil pesto

2 tablespoons white wine vinegar

1 teaspoon salt

1. In large bowl, toss beans, cucumber, tomato and onion.

2. In small bowl, mix pesto, vinegar and salt until well blended. Pour over bean mixture; toss until salad is coated with basil mixture.

3. Cover and refrigerate 1 hour or until serving.

1 Serving: Calories 140 (Calories from Fat 25); Total Fat 3g (Saturated Fat 0g); Cholesterol 0mg; Sodium 310mg; Total Carbohydrate 24g (Dietary Fiber 6g; Sugars 2g); Protein 8g

% Daily Value: Vitamin A 4%; Vitamin C 8%; Calcium 6%; Iron 15%

Exchanges: 1 1/2 Starch, 1/2 Very Lean Meat, 1/2 Fat

Carbohydrate Choices: 1

Once my kids hit third grade they didn't get recess anymore (except whatever time they have left after eating lunch), and they were coming home with only 3,000 steps for the day. So we have to work harder to be active at home.

Deb M.

Texas Coleslaw

Prep Time: 15 Minutes   Start to Finish: 1 Hour 15 Minutes

16 servings (1/2 cup each)

1 bag (16 oz) coleslaw mix
(shredded cabbage and carrots)

1/2 cup chopped fresh cilantro

2 cans (11 oz each) whole kernel corn
with red and green peppers, drained

1/4 cup canola or soybean oil

3 tablespoons lime or lemon juice

3/4 teaspoon ground cumin

1/2 teaspoon salt

1. In very large (4-quart) bowl, toss coleslaw mix, cilantro and corn. In tightly covered container, shake oil, lime juice, cumin and salt. Pour over coleslaw mixture; toss.

2. Cover and refrigerate 1 to 2 hours to blend flavors.

note from Dr. H:

Sit down to dinner together. In this hurry-up world, having great recipes to choose from, modeling smart eating habits and planning simple, healthy menus, as well as eating together, are key components to weight management success.

1 Serving: Calories 70 (Calories from Fat 35); Total Fat 3.5g (Saturated Fat 0g); Cholesterol 0mg; Sodium 85mg; Total Carbohydrate 8g (Dietary Fiber 2g; Sugars 2g); Protein 1g

% Daily Value: Vitamin A 30%; Vitamin C 20%; Calcium 0%; Iron 2%

Exchanges: 1 1/2 Vegetable, 1/2 Fat

Carbohydrate Choices: 1/2

Peanutty Pear Salad

Prep Time: 10 Minutes   Start to Finish: 10 Minutes

6 servings (1 1/2 cups each)

SOY-DIJON VINAIGRETTE

2 tablespoons olive or canola oil

1 tablespoon lemon juice

2 teaspoons sugar

2 teaspoons soy sauce

1 teaspoon Dijon mustard

SALAD

6 cups bite-size pieces mixed salad greens

2 large or 3 medium unpeeled ripe pears, sliced

1/3 cup dry-roasted peanuts

1/3 cup golden raisins

1. In tightly covered container, shake all vinaigrette ingredients.

2. Divide salad greens among 6 plates. Top with pears, peanuts and raisins. Drizzle with vinaigrette. Serve immediately.

1 Serving: Calories 170 (Calories from Fat 80); Total Fat 9g (Saturated Fat 1g); Cholesterol 0mg; Sodium 200mg; Total Carbohydrate 22g (Dietary Fiber 4g; Sugars 15g); Protein 4g

% Daily Value: Vitamin A 35%; Vitamin C 20%; Calcium 4%; Iron 8%

Exchanges: 1/2 Fruit, 1 1/2 Other Carbohydrate, 1/2 High-Fat Meat, 1 Fat

Carbohydrate Choices: 1 1/2

Mixed-Fruit Salad

Prep Time: 10 Minutes   **Start to Finish:** 10 Minutes

12 servings (1/2 cup each)

1 cup vanilla fat-free yogurt

1 tablespoon mayonnaise or salad dressing

1/4 teaspoon grated orange peel

2 tablespoons orange juice

6 cups cut-up assorted fresh fruits (melon, berries, grapes)

1. In large bowl, mix yogurt, mayonnaise, orange peel and orange juice.

2. Gently stir in fruit. Store covered in refrigerator.

note from DR. H:

Make physical activity a priority for yourself and your family by marking it on your calendar. When you commit to your well-being, other things will be less likely to get in the way. The time you spend being active is a wise investment.

We are trying to get into healthy habits. One that helps us all feel better is to drink more water every day. Now we pack water and take it with us wherever we go.

Steve O.

1 Serving: Calories 70 (Calories from Fat 10); Total Fat 1.5g (Saturated Fat 0g); Cholesterol 0mg; Sodium 20mg; Total Carbohydrate 13g (Dietary Fiber 0g; Sugars 11g); Protein 1g

% Daily Value: Vitamin A 15%; Vitamin C 50%; Calcium 4%; Iron 0%

Exchanges: 1 Fruit

Carbohydrate Choices: 1

Wiggly Jiggly Fruit Salad

Prep Time: 20 Minutes   **Start to Finish:** 2 Hours 20 Minutes

8 servings (1/2 cup each)

note from DR. H:

This terrific side has all the goodness of fruit, along with the fun of gelatin. Cooking and eating dinner together is a happy, wholesome way to create homemade fun.

3/4 cup boiling water

1 package (0.3 oz) strawberry-flavored sugar-free gelatin

1/4 cup 99% fat-free strawberry yogurt (from 6-oz container)

1 medium banana, sliced

1 can (8 oz) pineapple chunks in unsweetened juice, drained

1 1/2 cups sliced fresh strawberries

1. In small bowl, pour boiling water over gelatin; stir about 2 minutes or until gelatin is completely dissolved. Stir in yogurt until smooth. Refrigerate at least 2 hours until firm.

2. Dip bottom of bowl into very warm water about 15 seconds or until gelatin is loosened. Cut gelatin into 1-inch squares. Remove gelatin squares from bowl; place in serving bowl.

3. Add remaining ingredients to gelatin; toss gently.

1 Serving: Calories 50 (Calories from Fat 0); Total Fat 0g (Saturated Fat 0g); Cholesterol 0mg; Sodium 30mg; Total Carbohydrate 11g (Dietary Fiber 1g; Sugars 8g); Protein 1g

% Daily Value: Vitamin A 0%; Vitamin C 35%; Calcium 2%; Iron 0%

Exchanges: 1 Other Carbohydrate

Carbohydrate Choices: 1

Wow—who knew that sugar-free gelatin tastes as good as gelatin with sugar? It's easy to make a change like that, and save lots of calories.

Elizabeth H. age 8

Primavera Pasta Salad

Prep Time: 25 Minutes   **Start to Finish:** 25 Minutes

14 servings (3/4 cup each)

3 1/2 cups uncooked bow-tie
(farfalle) pasta (9 oz)

2 cups snow (Chinese) pea pods
(12 oz), strings removed

2 large red bell peppers, cut into
1-inch pieces (2 cups)

2 medium carrots, sliced (1 cup)

1/2 cup chopped fresh basil leaves

1/2 cup shredded
Parmesan cheese (2 oz)

1 cup reduced-fat creamy
Parmesan dressing

2 tablespoons milk

1. Cook and drain pasta as directed on package,
adding pea pods for last minute of cooking.
Rinse with cold water; drain.

2. In very large (4-quart) bowl, mix bell peppers,
carrots, basil and cheese. In small bowl, mix
dressing and milk with wire whisk. Add dressing
mixture, pasta and pea pods to bell pepper mixture;
toss to coat.

note from DR. H:

Don't be a member of
the "Clean Plate Club."
Encouraging kids to
finish all the food on
their plate teaches them
to eat visually instead of
going by their own full
or hunger cues.

1 Serving: Calories 150 (Calories
from Fat 25); Total Fat 3g
(Saturated Fat 1g); Cholesterol
0mg; Sodium 400mg; Total
Carbohydrate 26g (Dietary
Fiber 2g; Sugars 2g); Protein 7g

% Daily Value: Vitamin A 50%;
Vitamin C 50%; Calcium 8%;
Iron 8%

Exchanges: 1 1/2 Starch, 1/2 Fat

Carbohydrate Choices: 2

Get Kids Excited About Veggies and Fruits

Increasing the number of fruits and vegetables you eat has many benefits: eating a diet rich in veggies and fruits can lower your risk of heart disease, certain cancers and diabetes. Aim for at least five servings of veggies and fruits a day. But how do you get your kids to eat vegetables? Try these surefire ways:

Keep cut-up carrots, celery, cucumbers, radishes, bell peppers and cherry or grape tomatoes on hand for snacking.

Top baked potatoes and burgers with salsa. Make creamy salsa by mixing equal amounts of plain low-fat yogurt and salsa; use as a dip.

Let kids dunk veggies into a favorite low-fat or fat-free dressing.

Turn soups and salads into funny faces by topping with shredded lettuce, carrot or radishes for hair and using sliced green or ripe olives for eyes.

Encourage kids to "play" with their food. Cut carrots and celery into coins, broccoli and cauliflower into trees and forests.

Load sandwiches with sliced cucumbers, tomatoes, onions, bell peppers, lettuce or other vegetables.

Toss pasta with their favorites—corn, peas, green beans or carrots—before topping with sauce.

Stir green beans, shredded carrots or corn into soups, stews and casseroles. When you make lasagna, layer vegetables in with the other ingredients.

Try marinated vegetables (see Marinated Carrot Salad, page 210, and Dilly Beans, page 90).

Enjoy tomato and pasta sauces, tomato soup and ketchup. It counts!

Eat veggies yourself.

To get your kids to eat more fruit:

Layer a parfait with strawberries or other fruit, crushed cereal and yogurt.

Blend a smoothie using chopped fresh fruit, ice and plain fat-free yogurt.

Top cereal, pancakes, waffles and French toast with fruit.

Sprinkle fresh berries or sliced citrus fruits onto your salad.

Freeze grapes, strawberries and banana chunks and eat.

Eat fresh or canned fruit as a snack or for dessert.

Garlic Oven Fries

Prep Time: 10 Minutes   Start to Finish: 30 Minutes

4 servings (8 fries each)

4 medium red potatoes
(2 1/2 to 3 inch), each cut in 8 wedges

2 teaspoons olive or canola oil

1 teaspoon dried basil leaves

1 teaspoon garlic salt

1. Heat oven to 500°F. Spray 15x10x1-inch pan with cooking spray. In medium bowl, toss potatoes with oil to coat. Sprinkle with basil and garlic salt. Arrange in single layer in pan.

2. Bake uncovered 15 to 18 minutes, stirring once, until potatoes are tender but crisp on outside.

note from the nutritionist:

You can have the flavor of French-fried potatoes without all of the fat by coating the potatoes with just a little oil and roasting them at a high oven temperature.

1 Serving: Calories 130 (Calories from Fat 20); Total Fat 2.5g (Saturated Fat 0g); Cholesterol 0mg; Sodium 250mg; Total Carbohydrate 26g (Dietary Fiber 3g; Sugars 1g); Protein 2g

% Daily Value: Vitamin A 0%; Vitamin C 15%; Calcium 4%; Iron 15%

Exchanges: 1 1/2 Starch, 1/2 Fat

Carbohydrate Choices: 2

Four-Cheese Mashed Potato Casserole

Prep Time: 25 Minutes   **Start to Finish:** 1 Hour 35 Minutes

24 servings (1/2 cup each)

5 lb white potatoes, peeled, cut into 1-inch pieces (about 14 cups)

3 oz (from 8-oz package) reduced-fat cream cheese (Neufchâtel), softened

1/4 cup crumbled blue cheese

1 cup shredded reduced-fat Cheddar cheese (4 oz)

1/4 cup shredded Parmesan cheese

1 container (8 oz) reduced-fat sour cream

1 teaspoon garlic salt

milk (optional)

1/4 teaspoon paprika

1 teaspoon chopped fresh chives, if desired

1. In 6-quart saucepan or Dutch oven, place potatoes. Add enough water to cover potatoes. Heat to boiling over high heat; reduce heat to medium. Cook uncovered 15 to 18 minutes or until tender; drain. Mash potatoes in saucepan with potato masher or electric mixer on low speed.

2. Meanwhile, in large bowl, beat cream cheese, blue cheese, Cheddar cheese and Parmesan cheese with electric mixer on low speed until smooth. Beat in sour cream and garlic salt.

3. Heat oven to 350°F. Stir cheese mixture into mashed potatoes until well blended. If potatoes are too stiff, stir in milk, 1 tablespoon at a time, until desired consistency. Spoon into ungreased 13x9-inch (3-quart) glass baking dish.

4. Bake uncovered 35 to 40 minutes or until hot and top is lightly browned. Sprinkle with paprika and chives.

1 Serving: Calories 110 (Calories from Fat 25); Total Fat 3g (Saturated Fat 2g); Cholesterol 10mg; Sodium 140mg; Total Carbohydrate 18g (Dietary Fiber 2g; Sugars 1g); Protein 4g

% Daily Value: Vitamin A 4%; Vitamin C 6%; Calcium 8%; Iron 2%

Exchanges: 1 Starch, 1/2 Fat

Carbohydrate Choices: 1

Four-Cheese Mashed Potato Casserole

Pineapple-Topped Sweet Potatoes

Prep Time: 5 Minutes   **Start to Finish:** 1 Hour 15 Minutes

4 servings (1/2 potato each)

2 medium dark-orange
sweet potatoes

1/4 cup drained crushed pineapple in
juice (from 8-oz can)

1 tablespoon sunflower nuts

2 tablespoons packed brown sugar

1. Heat oven to 375°F. Scrub potatoes; prick all over
with fork. Place in shallow baking pan or pie pan
(do not use glass). Bake 55 to 65 minutes or until
tender.

2. Set oven control to broil. Cut potatoes lengthwise
in half. Mash cut sides slightly with fork. Spoon
pineapple over cut sides of potatoes. Top with
sunflower nuts and brown sugar.

3. Broil with tops 4 to 6 inches from heat 2 to 3 minutes
or until brown sugar is bubbly.

1 Serving: Calories 110 (Calories
from Fat 10); Total Fat 1.5g
(Saturated Fat 0g); Cholesterol
0mg; Sodium 20mg; Total
Carbohydrate 25g (Dietary Fiber
2g; Sugars 18g); Protein 2g

% Daily Value: Vitamin A 200%;
Vitamin C 15%; Calcium 2%;
Iron 4%

Exchanges: 1/2 Starch,
1 Other Carbohydrate, 1/2 Fat

Carbohydrate Choices: 1 1/2

Pineapple-Topped Sweet Potatoes

Streusel-Topped Squash

Prep Time: 20 Minutes   Start to Finish: 1 Hour 5 Minutes

8 servings (1/2 cup each)

1 butternut squash (2 to 2 1/2 lb), peeled, seeded and cut into 1/2-inch cubes (about 4 1/2 cups)

1/4 cup water

1/2 teaspoon salt

1/3 cup all-purpose flour

1/4 cup packed brown sugar

1/4 cup chopped pecans

2 tablespoons butter or margarine, softened

1/2 teaspoon pumpkin pie spice

1. Heat oven to 350°F. In 11x7-inch microwavable dish, spread squash cubes. Add water; sprinkle with salt. Cover with plastic wrap, folding back one edge or corner 1/4 inch to vent steam. Microwave on High about 5 minutes or until squash is crisp-tender.

2. Meanwhile, in medium bowl, mix remaining ingredients with spoon. Sprinkle evenly over squash.

3. Bake uncovered 40 to 45 minutes or until streusel is brown.

note from DR. H:

This recipe is a great way to get kids to try squash. Offer variety, because kids need to try new and different foods. Yet, it may take up to several times of trying a new food until they decide they like it.

1 Serving: Calories 130 (Calories from Fat 50); Total Fat 6g (Saturated Fat 1.5g); Cholesterol 10mg; Sodium 190mg; Total Carbohydrate 18g (Dietary Fiber 1g; Sugars 9g); Protein 2g

% Daily Value: Vitamin A 120%; Vitamin C 8%; Calcium 4%; Iron 4%

Exchanges: 1 Starch, 1 Fat

Carbohydrate Choices: 1

" *You can watch TV and walk on the treadmill, too. Exercise can be fun!* "
Clarke S. age 9

Carrots with Parsley Butter

Prep Time: 10 Minutes   Start to Finish: 25 Minutes

4 servings (1/2 cup each)

2 cups baby-cut carrots

1/2 cup chicken broth

1 tablespoon sugar

2 teaspoons butter or margarine

1 teaspoon cornstarch

1 tablespoon cold water

1 tablespoon chopped fresh parsley

1. In 1 1/2-quart saucepan, heat carrots and broth to boiling over high heat; reduce heat. Cover and simmer about 8 minutes or until tender. Remove carrots from liquid; place in small bowl and cover to keep warm.

2. Stir sugar and butter into liquid in saucepan until butter is melted and sugar is dissolved. In small bowl, mix cornstarch and water; stir into butter mixture in saucepan. Heat to boiling, about 1 minute, until slightly thickened.

3. Pour butter mixture over carrots. Add parsley; toss.

note from DR. H:

Go ahead, take the 10 minutes or so while the carrots are simmering to be active with the kids. Shoot a few hoops or toss a ball—setting a good example sends a powerful message to your kids.

1 Serving: Calories 60 (Calories from Fat 20); Total Fat 2g (Saturated Fat 1g); Cholesterol 5mg; Sodium 160mg; Total Carbohydrate 10g (Dietary Fiber 2g; Sugars 6g); Protein 1g

% Daily Value: Vitamin A 230%; Vitamin C 6%; Calcium 0%; Iron 2%

Exchanges: 1 Vegetable, 1/2 Fat

Carbohydrate Choices: 1/2

Marinated Carrot Salad

Prep Time: 20 Minutes   Start to Finish: 24 Hours 45 Minutes

8 servings (1/2 cup each)

2 cups water

1 lb baby-cut carrots, cut crosswise in half

1 medium onion, chopped (1/2 cup)

1 medium red bell pepper, cut into bite-size pieces

1 medium stalk celery, cut into 1/2-inch slices (1/2 cup)

1 can (10 3/4 oz) condensed tomato soup

1/3 cup honey

1/3 cup cider vinegar

1 tablespoon canola or soybean oil

1 teaspoon Dijon mustard

1/2 teaspoon salt

1/4 teaspoon pepper

1. In 2-quart saucepan, heat water and carrots to boiling; reduce heat. Simmer uncovered 8 to 11 minutes or just until crisp-tender; drain.

2. In large bowl, toss carrots, onion, bell pepper and celery.

3. In 1-quart saucepan, mix remaining ingredients. Heat to boiling. Pour over vegetables; toss gently.

4. Cover and refrigerate 24 hours before serving.

note from DR. H:

The beauty of this recipe is that it's prepared ahead of time and has a couple of steps—the perfect recipe to get the crew involved. Everyone can take a role, from washing the carrots, to cutting the vegetables to stirring the marinade.

1 Serving: Calories 120 (Calories from Fat 20); Total Fat 2.5g (Saturated Fat 0g); Cholesterol 0mg; Sodium 420mg; Total Carbohydrate 26g (Dietary Fiber 3g; Sugars 19g); Protein 1g

% Daily Value: Vitamin A 230%; Vitamin C 35%; Calcium 2%; Iron 4%

Exchanges: 1 1/2 Other Carbohydrate, 1 Vegetable, 1/2 Fat

Carbohydrate Choices: 2

Scalloped Corn

Prep Time: 20 Minutes   **Start to Finish:** 35 Minutes

4 servings (1/2 cup each)

1 tablespoon butter or margarine

1 small onion, finely chopped (1/4 cup)

1/4 cup finely chopped green bell pepper

1 tablespoon all-purpose flour

1/2 teaspoon salt

1/4 teaspoon ground mustard

Dash of pepper

2/3 cup fat-free (skim) milk

1 can (15.25 oz) whole-kernel corn, drained

1 cup Country® Corn Flakes cereal

1 tablespoon butter or margarine, melted

1. Heat oven to 350°F. In 10-inch skillet, melt 1 tablespoon butter over medium heat. Cook onion and bell pepper in butter 4 to 6 minutes, stirring occasionally, until crisp-tender.

2. Stir in flour, salt, mustard and pepper. Cook 1 to 2 minutes, stirring constantly, until smooth and well mixed; remove from heat.

3. Stir in milk. Heat to boiling, stirring constantly; boil and stir 1 minute. Stir in corn. Pour into ungreased 1-quart casserole.

4. In small bowl, mix cereal and 1 tablespoon melted butter; sprinkle over corn mixture. Bake uncovered 10 to 15 minutes or until mixture is bubbly and topping is golden.

note from the nutritionist:

Is there any vegetable that kids love more than corn? Corn has fiber and other nutrients. If you like, you can even make this tasty side dish into a main-dish casserole that serves four by adding 1 1/2 cups diced cooked chicken, turkey or ham.

1 Serving: Calories 190 (Calories from Fat 60); Total Fat 7g (Saturated Fat 3g); Cholesterol 15mg; Sodium 630mg; Total Carbohydrate 30g (Dietary Fiber 3g; Sugars 6g); Protein 5g

% Daily Value: Vitamin A 10%; Vitamin C 15%; Calcium 10%; Iron 15%

Exchanges: 2 Starch, 1 Fat

Carbohydrate Choices: 2

Broccoli, Pepper and Bacon Toss

Prep Time: 15 Minutes   Start to Finish: 15 Minutes

6 servings (1/2 cup each)

1 bag (14 oz) frozen broccoli florets

2 cups frozen stir-fry bell peppers and onions (from 1-lb bag)

1/2 cup raisins

2 tablespoons reduced-fat coleslaw dressing

2 tablespoons real bacon pieces (from 2.8-oz package)

1. Cook broccoli and stir-fry bell peppers and onions mixture separately in microwave as directed on packages. Drain well.

2. In large bowl, toss broccoli, bell pepper mixture, raisins and coleslaw dressing. Sprinkle with bacon. Serve warm.

note from the nutritionist:

Broccoli is in the cruciferous family of vegetables. Along with cabbage, Brussels sprouts and cauliflower, it's a nutrient powerhouse. Cruciferous vegetables are thought to protect against diseases, particularly cancer.

1 Serving: Calories 100 (Calories from Fat 20); Total Fat 2.5g (Saturated Fat 0.5g); Cholesterol 0mg; Sodium 135mg; Total Carbohydrate 19g (Dietary Fiber 3g; Sugars 11g); Protein 3g

% Daily Value: Vitamin A 20%; Vitamin C 70%; Calcium 4%; Iron 6%

Exchanges: 1 Other Carbohydrate, 1 Vegetable, 1/2 Fat

Carbohydrate Choices: 1

Broccoli, Pepper and Bacon Toss

Oven-Roasted Italian Vegetables

Prep Time: 10 Minutes   **Start to Finish:** 40 Minutes

8 servings (3/4 cup each)

1 1/2 cups baby-cut carrots (8 oz)

1 1/2 cups fresh whole mushrooms (4 oz)

2 medium onions, cut into 1-inch wedges (2 cups)

1 large red bell pepper, cut into 1-inch pieces (2 cups)

1 medium zucchini, cut lengthwise in half, then cut crosswise into 1-inch slices (1 cup)

3 small red potatoes, cut into fourths (1 cup)

1/2 cup fat-free Italian dressing

1. Heat oven to 450°F. Generously spray 15x10x1-inch pan with cooking spray. In large bowl, toss vegetables with dressing. Spread vegetables in single layer in pan.

2. Bake uncovered about 30 minutes, stirring occasionally, until crisp-tender.

1 Serving: Calories 50 (Calories from Fat 0); Total Fat 0g (Saturated Fat 0g); Cholesterol 0mg; Sodium 170mg; Total Carbohydrate 13g (Dietary Fiber 3g; Sugars 6g); Protein 2g

% Daily Value: Vitamin A 110%; Vitamin C 45%; Calcium 2%; Iron 4%

Exchanges: 1/2 Starch, 1 Vegetable

Carbohydrate Choices: 1

Oven-'fried' chicken and fish are appealing substitutes for the traditional frying. Oven-baked French fries are a household favorite.

Greg S.

Italian Cauliflower

Prep Time: 10 Minutes **Start to Finish:** 10 Minutes

6 servings (1/2 cup each)

4 cups fresh cauliflowerets

2 tablespoons water

2 teaspoons olive or canola oil

2 tablespoons Italian-style dry bread crumbs

1 teaspoon dried basil leaves

1 tablespoon chopped fresh parsley

1. In medium microwavable bowl, cover and microwave cauliflower and water on High about 6 minutes, stirring once after 3 minutes, until tender; drain.

2. Meanwhile, in 7-inch skillet, heat oil over medium heat. Stir in bread crumbs and basil. Cook 1 to 2 minutes, stirring frequently, until bread crumbs are toasted. Stir in parsley. Sprinkle over cauliflower.

note from the nutritionist:

Toasting the bread crumbs in a skillet provides a wonderful toasty flavor without having to use the broiler. You can reduce the amount of saturated fat in your diet by using olive or canola oil instead of butter like this tasty side dish does.

1 Serving: Calories 40 (Calories from Fat 15); Total Fat 2g (Saturated Fat 0g); Cholesterol 0mg; Sodium 40mg; Total Carbohydrate 5g (Dietary Fiber 2g; Sugars 2g); Protein 2g

% Daily Value: Vitamin A 4%; Vitamin C 25%; Calcium 2%; Iron 4%

Exchanges: 1 Vegetable, 1/2 Fat

Carbohydrate Choices: 1

Grilled Seasoned Sage Potato Packet

Prep Time: 10 Minutes   **Start to Finish:** 1 Hour

8 servings (about 1/2 cup each)

4 small unpeeled red potatoes, cut into fourths (about 1 1/2 cups)

2 medium unpeeled russet potatoes, cut into 1-inch chunks (about 2 cups)

2 tablespoons firm butter or margarine

1/2 teaspoon dried sage leaves

1/2 teaspoon paprika

1/2 teaspoon seasoned salt

2 tablespoons chopped fresh chives

1. Heat coals or gas grill for direct heat. Cut 18x12-inch piece of heavy-duty foil; spray with cooking spray. Place potatoes on foil. Cut butter into small pieces; sprinkle over potatoes. Sprinkle with sage, paprika and seasoned salt.

2. Fold foil over potatoes so edges meet. Seal edges, making tight 1/2-inch fold; fold again. Allow space on sides for circulation and expansion.

3. Cover and grill packet over medium heat 40 to 50 minutes, rotating packet 1/2 turn after about 20 minutes, until potatoes are tender. Cut large X across top of packet; fold back foil. Sprinkle with chives.

1 Serving: Calories 80 (Calories from Fat 25); Total Fat 3g (Saturated Fat 1.5g); Cholesterol 10mg; Sodium 110mg; Total Carbohydrate 12g (Dietary Fiber 2g; Sugars 0g); Protein 1g

% Daily Value: Vitamin A 4%; Vitamin C 6%; Calcium 0%; Iron 6%

Exchanges: 1 Starch, 1/2 Fat

Carbohydrate Choices: 1

Grilled Parmesan Potatoes

Prep Time: 10 Minutes   Start to Finish: 35 Minutes

4 servings (1/2 packet each)

4 medium potatoes, thinly sliced

1/2 teaspoon salt

1/4 cup Italian-style bread crumbs

2 tablespoons grated
Parmesan cheese

2 tablespoons butter or
margarine, melted

1 tablespoon chopped fresh or
1 teaspoon dried basil leaves

1. Heat coals or gas grill for direct heat. Cut two 30x18-inch sheets of heavy-duty foil.

2. Divide potato slices between foil sheets. Sprinkle with salt. In small bowl, mix remaining ingredients; sprinkle over potatoes. Wrap foil securely around potatoes; pierce top of foil once or twice with fork to vent steam.

3. Cover and grill foil packets, seam side up, over medium heat 18 to 23 minutes, rotating packets once, until potatoes are tender. Place packets on plates; unfold foil.

To Bake: Heat oven to 450°F. Prepare packets as directed. Bake 25 to 30 minutes or until potatoes are tender. Place packets on plates; unfold foil.

note from the nutritionist:

Because of their simple, fresh flavor, these potatoes are a perfect accompaniment to grilled steak, pork chops or chicken. If you are trying to keep the fat even lower, you can reduce the butter and Parmesan cheese to 1 tablespoon each.

1 Serving: Calories 200 (Calories from Fat 60); Total Fat 7g (Saturated Fat 3.5g); Cholesterol 20mg; Sodium 460mg; Total Carbohydrate 30g (Dietary Fiber 4g; Sugars 2g); Protein 4g

% Daily Value: Vitamin A 6%; Vitamin C 15%; Calcium 10%; Iron 15%

Exchanges: 2 Starch, 1 Fat

Carbohydrate Choices: 2

Mixed-Berry Cream Tart (page 238)

SAVE ROOM FOR DESSERT

Tropical Fruit Dip with Cookies and Fruit

Prep Time: 15 Minutes   Start to Finish: 15 Minutes

8 servings

1 cup vanilla fat-free yogurt

1/4 cup flaked coconut, toasted if desired

1 can (8 oz) crushed pineapple in juice, drained

2 tablespoons packed brown sugar

2 nectarines, sliced

16 strawberries

8 small bunches grapes

16 gingersnaps or graham cracker squares

1. In small bowl, mix yogurt, coconut, pineapple and brown sugar.

2. Serve dip immediately with fruit and gingersnaps, or cover and refrigerate at least 1 hour.

note from the nutritionist:

With this tasty tropical dip, you can have your dip, fruit and cookies, too! You can use any fresh fruit, but keep about the same amounts for portion control.

1 Serving: Calories 180 (Calories from Fat 25); Total Fat 2.5g (Saturated Fat 1g); Cholesterol 0mg; Sodium 105mg; Total Carbohydrate 38g (Dietary Fiber 2g; Sugars 30g); Protein 3g

% Daily Value: Vitamin A 2%; Vitamin C 40%; Calcium 6%; Iron 4%

Exchanges: 1 Starch, 1 Fruit, 1/2 Other Carbohydrate, 1/2 Fat

Carbohydrate Choices: 2 1/2

Every night at dinner we ask each person, 'What was your best thing today?' and 'What was your worst thing today?' Everyone gets their turn and gets to hear about the others' day. It is a great conversation starter. My kids (6, 8 and 10) get really excited to share.

Deb M.

Tropical Fruit Dip with Cookies and Fruit

Raspberry-Lemon Fruit Dip

Prep Time: 15 Minutes   **Start to Finish:** 15 Minutes

20 servings (1 tablespoon dip and 3 fruit pieces each)

1/2 cup raspberry reduced-fat cream cheese spread (from 8-oz container), softened

1/2 cup marshmallow creme

1 container (6 oz) lemon fat-free yogurt (2/3 cup)

Assorted fresh fruit

1. In medium bowl, mix cream cheese and marshmallow creme with wire whisk until smooth. Stir in yogurt.

2. Serve dip with fruit.

1 Serving: Calories 60 (Calories from Fat 10); Total Fat 1g (Saturated Fat 0.5g); Cholesterol 0mg; Sodium 40mg; Total Carbohydrate 12g (Dietary Fiber 0g; Sugars 8g); Protein 1g

% Daily Value: Vitamin A 0%; Vitamin C 15%; Calcium 2%; Iron 0%

Exchanges: 1/2 Fruit, 1/2 Other Carbohydrate

Carbohydrate Choices: 1

Be Good to Your Health with Smart Fats

Studies show that some fat is essential for everyone, so don't worry, fats aren't all bad! A good goal: Limit your calories from fat to no more than 30 percent of total calories, and keep saturated fat calories to no more than 10 percent of total calories.

How much fat should I eat every day?

To estimate how many total grams of fat to aim for, multiply your daily calorie level by 30 percent and divide by 9. For example, if you need 2,000 calories per day: 2,000 calories x 0.3 = 600 calories. 600 calories/9 calories per gram of fat = 67 grams.

The good news: Using canola, olive, soybean and other vegetable oils can benefit your health. Replacing some saturated-fat foods with poly- and monounsaturated-fat foods will help improve your ratio of "protective" cholesterol to "harmful" cholesterol.

To add monounsaturated (good) fats to your diet:

Snack on walnuts, soy nuts, almonds and peanuts. Add nuts to salads, stir-fries, snacks and desserts.

Cook and bake with canola, soybean or olive oil.

Snack on small amounts of avocados and olives, or top salads and casseroles with them.

Eat fatty fish, especially salmon, sardines, bluefish and albacore tuna, once or twice a week.

To lower overall fat and saturated fat:

Eat smaller portions. Skip the super-size meals and snacks, and choose normal-size servings. Fill up on fruits and vegetables if you are still hungry.

Trim visible fat from meat and remove skin from chicken and turkey before eating.

Cook lean. Broil, bake, roast, grill, poach, steam, stew or microwave foods whenever possible.

Select lean chicken, turkey, fish and meat. Buy the leanest cuts of chicken, turkey, beef and fish. They are naturally low in fat if you remove the skin.

Go meatless a couple of times each week. To reduce saturated fat and increase fiber and complex carbohydrates, limit the amount of meat and poultry you eat. Try dishes made with dried beans and peas, grains, fruits and vegetables.

Choose reduced-fat mayonnaise, salad dressings and sour cream. The amount of fat in creamy dressings adds up fast, so use reduced-fat varieties whenever possible.

Use fat-free or reduced-fat dairy products. Drink fat-free (skim) milk and use fat-free or reduced-fat yogurt, cottage cheese, cheese, pudding and ice cream.

Go easy on butter, margarine and cream sauces. Use tub margarine as a spread, canola oil or butter in baking and cream sauces only once in a great while.

Cut back on trans fats in potato or other chips, French fries, high-fat cheeses, doughnuts, muffins and cookies. Instead, eat lower-fat microwave popcorn, whole-grain tortilla chips, pretzels and other lower-fat snacks.

Read labels. Nutrition labels tell you how much fat, saturated fat and trans fats each food contains.

Indulge in fresh fruits and vegetables. Evidence indicates that eating a diet rich in many veggies and fruits can lower the risk of heart disease.

Blueberry Cake Bars

Prep Time: 15 Minutes   **Start to Finish:** 1 Hour 45 Minutes

24 bars

CRUMB TOPPING

1/3 cup all-purpose flour

1/3 cup granulated sugar

1/2 teaspoon ground cinnamon

1/8 teaspoon ground cardamom, if desired

3 tablespoons firm butter or margarine

BARS

1 cup granulated sugar

1/3 cup butter or margarine, softened

1/4 cup fat-free buttermilk

2 eggs or 1/2 cup fat-free egg product

1 1/4 cups all-purpose flour

1 teaspoon baking powder

1/8 teaspoon salt

1 cup frozen blueberries (from 16-oz bag), thawed, drained

1. Heat oven to 350°F. Grease bottom only of 13x9-inch pan with shortening or spray with cooking spray. In medium bowl, mix 1/3 cup flour, 1/3 cup granulated sugar, the cinnamon and cardamom. Cut in 3 tablespoons butter, using pastry blender (or pulling 2 table knives through ingredients in opposite directions), until mixture is crumbly; set aside.

2. In large bowl, beat 1 cup granulated sugar and 1/3 cup butter with electric mixer on medium speed until creamy. Beat in buttermilk and eggs on low speed until smooth. Beat in 1 1/4 cups flour, the baking powder and salt. Spread in pan. Sprinkle with blueberries and topping.

3. Bake 25 to 30 minutes or until toothpick inserted in center comes out clean. Cool completely, about 1 hour. For bars, cut into 6 rows by 4 rows.

1 Bar: Calories 120 (Calories from Fat 40); Total Fat 4.5g (Saturated Fat 2g); Cholesterol 30mg; Sodium 70mg; Total Carbohydrate 19g (Dietary Fiber 0g; Sugars 12g); Protein 2g

% Daily Value: Vitamin A 4%; Vitamin C 0%; Calcium 2%; Iron 2%

Exchanges: 1/2 Starch, 1/2 Other Carbohydrate, 1 Fat

Carbohydrate Choices: 1

Exercise: Do crunches and walk—on the weekends, in the morning, whenever you think of it.
Clarke S. age 9

Blueberry Cake Bars

Raspberry-Chocolate Bars

Prep Time: 20 Minutes   **Start to Finish:** 3 Hours 20 Minutes

48 bars

1 1/2 cups all-purpose flour

3/4 cup sugar

3/4 cup butter or margarine, softened

1 box (10 oz) frozen raspberries in syrup, thawed, undrained

1/4 cup orange juice

1 tablespoon cornstarch

3/4 cup miniature semisweet chocolate chips

1. Heat oven to 350°F. In medium bowl, beat flour, sugar and butter with electric mixer on medium speed, or mix with spoon. Press in bottom of ungreased 13x9-inch pan. Bake 15 minutes.

2. Meanwhile, in 1-quart saucepan, mix raspberries, orange juice and cornstarch. Heat to boiling, stirring constantly. Boil and stir 1 minute. Cool 10 minutes.

3. Sprinkle chocolate chips over baked layer. Spoon raspberry mixture over chocolate chips; spread carefully.

4. Bake about 20 minutes or until raspberry mixture is set. Cool 30 minutes. Refrigerate at least 1 hour for easier cutting. For bars, cut into 8 rows by 6 rows.

note from the nutritionist:

Studies show that trying to lose weight by depriving yourself doesn't work for very long, so go ahead and have a little treat once in a while. For a tangy kick in this recipe, try substituting cranberry juice for the orange juice to make Cran-Raspberry–Chocolate Bars.

1 Bar: Calories 70 (Calories from Fat 35); Total Fat 3.5g (Saturated Fat 2g); Cholesterol 10mg; Sodium 20mg; Total Carbohydrate 10g (Dietary Fiber 0g; Sugars 6g); Protein 0g

% Daily Value: Vitamin A 2%; Vitamin C 0%; Calcium 0%; Iron 0%

Exchanges: 1/2 Other Carbohydrate, 1 Fat

Carbohydrate Choices: 1/2

Iced Lemon Shortbread Bars

Prep Time: 25 Minutes   Start to Finish: 2 Hours 10 Minutes

36 bars

BARS

3/4 cup powdered sugar

1/4 cup granulated sugar

1 cup butter or margarine, slightly softened

2 tablespoons grated lemon peel

1/4 cup lemon juice

2 1/4 cups all-purpose flour

1/3 cup cornstarch

1/4 teaspoon salt

LEMON ICING

2 cups powdered sugar

2 teaspoons light corn syrup

1 teaspoon grated lemon peel

3 to 4 tablespoons lemon juice

1. Heat oven to 325°F (if using dark or nonstick pan, heat oven to 300°F). Grease bottom and sides of 13x9-inch pan with shortening or spray with cooking spray.

2. In large bowl, beat 3/4 cup powdered sugar, the granulated sugar and butter with electric mixer on low speed until combined. Beat on medium speed until light and fluffy. Stir in 2 tablespoons lemon peel and 1/4 cup lemon juice. Stir in flour, cornstarch and salt. Press dough in pan with floured fingers.

3. Bake 35 to 45 minutes or until top is light golden brown. Cool completely, about 45 minutes.

4. In medium bowl, mix all icing ingredients with spoon until smooth and spreadable. Spread icing over bars; let stand about 15 minutes or until set. For bars, cut into 6 rows by 6 rows.

 We still make room for small treats.

Ruby O. age 9

note from the nutritionist:

All foods can be part of a healthy eating plan. The key is to enjoy them in moderate amounts, making sure to eat a wide variety of foods. One of these delicious lemon bars makes a great snack or dessert.

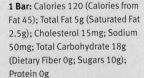

1 Bar: Calories 120 (Calories from Fat 45); Total Fat 5g (Saturated Fat 2.5g); Cholesterol 15mg; Sodium 50mg; Total Carbohydrate 18g (Dietary Fiber 0g; Sugars 10g); Protein 0g

% Daily Value: Vitamin A 4%; Vitamin C 0%; Calcium 0%; Iron 2%

Exchanges: 1 Other Carbohydrate, 1 Fat

Carbohydrate Choices: 1

Ginger Crinkles

Prep Time: 55 Minutes   **Start to Finish:** 55 Minutes

About 3 dozen cookies

1 cup sugar

3/4 cup butter or margarine, softened

1/4 cup molasses

1 egg or 1/4 cup fat-free egg product

2 cups all-purpose flour

1 tablespoon ground ginger

2 teaspoons baking soda

1 teaspoon ground cinnamon

1/4 teaspoon ground cloves

1/4 teaspoon salt

3 tablespoons sugar

1. Heat oven to 375°F. In large bowl, beat 1 cup sugar and the butter with electric mixer on medium speed, or mix with spoon, until soft and fluffy. Beat in molasses and egg. Stir in remaining ingredients except 3 tablespoons sugar until well blended.

2. Place 3 tablespoons sugar in small bowl. Shape dough by tablespoonfuls into balls; roll in sugar. On ungreased cookie sheet, place balls 2 inches apart.

3. Bake 6 to 8 minutes or until golden brown. Remove from cookie sheet to wire rack.

1 Cookie: Calories 100 (Calories from Fat 35); Total Fat 4g (Saturated Fat 2g); Cholesterol 15mg; Sodium 115mg; Total Carbohydrate 14g (Dietary Fiber 0g; Sugars 8g); Protein 0g

% Daily Value: Vitamin A 4%; Vitamin C 0%; Calcium 0%; Iron 2%

Exchanges: 1/2 Starch, 1/2 Other Carbohydrate, 1 Fat

Carbohydrate Choices: 1

Sassy Cinnamon Cookies

Prep Time: 25 Minutes   **Start to Finish:** 45 Minutes

About 3 dozen cookies

3/4 cup sugar

1/4 cup butter or margarine, softened

1/2 teaspoon vanilla

1 egg or 1/4 cup fat-free egg product

1 1/4 cups all-purpose flour

1/2 teaspoon cream of tartar

1/4 teaspoon baking soda

1/8 teaspoon salt

1/2 cup cinnamon-flavored baking chips

1/2 cup chopped pecans

2 tablespoons sugar

1 teaspoon ground cinnamon

1. Heat oven to 375°F (if using dark or nonstick pan, heat oven to 350°F). In large bowl, beat 3/4 cup sugar, the butter, vanilla and egg with electric mixer on medium speed, or mix with spoon, until creamy. Stir in flour, cream of tartar, baking soda and salt. Stir in cinnamon chips and pecans.

2. In small bowl, mix 2 tablespoons sugar and the cinnamon. Shape dough by tablespoonfuls into 1-inch balls. Roll balls in cinnamon-sugar. On ungreased cookie sheet, place balls 1 inch apart.

3. Bake 7 to 10 minutes or until set and light brown. Immediately remove from cookie sheet to wire rack.

note from DR. H:

Parents can be a positive influence on children by guiding them toward healthy food choices and active lifestyles and by nurturing them and setting the limits they need. When you are a role model to your children you not only help them, you help yourself as well.

Get the kids to make healthy choices early. Our children are 5 and 9 years old, and we typically ask them what they 'think' they want for a meal. Already, they look for balance in their meals. They still enjoy their high-fat favorites when they go to restaurants, friends' houses or even Grandma's house. But on a typical day, they have at least one opportunity to select healthy options.

Greg S.

2 Cookies: Calories 80 (Calories from Fat 30); Total Fat 3.5g (Saturated Fat 1g); Cholesterol 10mg; Sodium 35mg; Total Carbohydrate 10g (Dietary Fiber 0g; Sugars 7g); Protein 1g

% Daily Value: Vitamin A 0%; Vitamin C 0%; Calcium 0%; Iron 0%

Exchanges: 1/2 Other Carbohydrate, 1 Fat

Carbohydrate Choices: 1/2

Applesauce-Carrot Spice Cake

Prep Time: 25 Minutes **Start to Finish:** 2 Hours 25 Minutes

32 servings

note from DR. H:

Walking is one of the most popular forms of exercise in the world. Researchers have found that walking helps improve fitness, decreases blood pressure and reduces tension and anxiety to improve your mood.

CAKE

1 cup old-fashioned or quick-cooking oats

1 1/4 cups unsweetened applesauce

1 cup packed brown sugar

2 cups shredded carrots (about 4 medium)

2 eggs or 1/2 cup fat-free egg product

1/3 cup canola or soybean oil

1 1/2 cups whole wheat flour

2 teaspoons baking powder

1 teaspoon baking soda

1/2 teaspoon salt

1 tablespoon pumpkin pie spice

1/2 cup golden raisins

FROSTING

4 oz (from 8-oz package) reduced-fat cream cheese (Neufchâtel), softened

1/4 cup powdered sugar

3 tablespoons milk

1 teaspoon vanilla

1. Heat oven to 350°F. Spray 12-cup fluted tube cake pan with cooking spray.

2. In large bowl, mix oats, applesauce, brown sugar, carrots, eggs and oil with spoon until well mixed. Stir in remaining cake ingredients just until moistened. Pour into pan.

3. Bake 50 to 55 minutes or until toothpick inserted in center comes out clean. Cool in pan 10 minutes. Remove from pan to wire rack. Cool completely, about 1 hour.

4. In small bowl, beat cream cheese and powdered sugar with electric mixer on medium speed until smooth. Beat in milk and vanilla until well mixed. Spoon over cake.

1 Serving: Calories 110 (Calories from Fat 35); Total Fat 4g (Saturated Fat 1g); Cholesterol 15mg; Sodium 130mg; Total Carbohydrate 17g (Dietary Fiber 1g; Sugars 10g); Protein 2g

% Daily Value: Vitamin A 25%; Vitamin C 0%; Calcium 4%; Iron 4%

Exchanges: 1/2 Starch, 1/2 Other Carbohydrate, 1 Fat

Carbohydrate Choices: 1

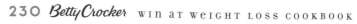

Applesauce-Carrot Spice Cake

Double Chocolate–Peanut Butter Cupcakes

Prep Time: 20 Minutes   Start to Finish: 1 Hour 10 Minutes

12 cupcakes

3/4 cup granulated sugar

3 tablespoons creamy peanut butter

1/4 cup fat-free sour cream

1 egg

1 egg white

1 cup all-purpose flour

1/4 cup baking cocoa

1/2 cup hot water

1/2 teaspoon baking soda

1/4 cup miniature semisweet chocolate chips

Powdered sugar, if desired

1. Heat oven to 350°F. Line 12 regular-size muffin cups with paper baking cups.

2. In large bowl, beat granulated sugar, peanut butter, sour cream, egg and egg white with electric mixer on medium speed until well blended. Beat in remaining ingredients except powdered sugar on low speed just until mixed. Divide among muffin cups.

3. Bake 15 to 20 minutes or until toothpick inserted in center comes out clean. Remove from pan to wire rack. Cool completely, about 30 minutes. Sprinkle tops with powdered sugar.

1 Cupcake: Calories 150 (Calories from Fat 35); Total Fat 4g (Saturated Fat 1.5g); Cholesterol 20mg; Sodium 90mg; Total Carbohydrate 25g (Dietary Fiber 1g; Sugars 15g); Protein 4g

% Daily Value: Vitamin A 0%; Vitamin C 0%; Calcium 0%; Iron 6%

Exchanges: 1/2 Starch, 1 Other Carbohydrate, 1 Fat

Carbohydrate Choices: 1 1/2

Caramel Pudding Cake

Prep Time: 20 Minutes   **Start to Finish:** 1 Hour 20 Minutes

9 servings

1 1/4 cups all-purpose flour

3/4 cup granulated sugar

1 1/2 teaspoons baking powder

1/2 teaspoon baking soda

1/4 teaspoon salt

1/2 cup fat-free buttermilk

2 tablespoons butter or margarine, melted

1/2 cup chopped dates, if desired

1/4 cup chopped nuts

3/4 cup packed brown sugar

1 1/2 cups very warm water (120°F to 130°F)

1. Heat oven to 350°F. In large bowl, mix flour, granulated sugar, baking powder, baking soda and salt with spoon. Stir in buttermilk and butter. Stir in dates and nuts (batter will be thick). In ungreased 8-inch or 9-inch square pan, spread batter.

2. In small bowl, mix brown sugar and very warm water with spoon. Pour over batter.

3. Bake 45 to 55 minutes or until cake is deep golden brown and toothpick inserted in center comes out clean. Serve warm.

note from DR. H:

Reward yourself. Keep track of your family achievements to remind yourselves how far you've come. When you achieve a goal, celebrate by treating yourself to a night out, a family game or another special event.

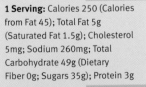

1 Serving: Calories 250 (Calories from Fat 45); Total Fat 5g (Saturated Fat 1.5g); Cholesterol 5mg; Sodium 260mg; Total Carbohydrate 49g (Dietary Fiber 0g; Sugars 35g); Protein 3g

% Daily Value: Vitamin A 2%; Vitamin C 0%; Calcium 8%; Iron 8%

Exchanges: 1 Starch, 2 Other Carbohydrate, 1 Fat

Carbohydrate Choices: 3

Chocolate Pudding with Marshmallows

Prep Time: 15 Minutes   Start to Finish: 15 Minutes

6 servings

note from the nutritionist:

Excite the kids with this easy, delicious pudding topped with mini marshmallows. To keep the fat and cholesterol lower, a combination of whole eggs, egg whites and skim milk is used. This pudding gives an extra boost of calcium, a mineral everyone needs.

2 eggs

2 egg whites

1/2 cup sugar

1/3 cup baking cocoa

2 tablespoons cornstarch

2 cups fat-free (skim) milk

1 tablespoon butter or margarine

1 teaspoon vanilla

1/2 cup miniature marshmallows

1. In medium bowl, slightly beat eggs and egg whites; set aside.

2. In 2-quart saucepan, mix sugar, cocoa and cornstarch. Gradually stir in milk. Cook over medium heat, stirring constantly with wire whisk, until mixture thickens and boils. Boil and stir 1 minute.

3. Gradually stir at least half of the hot mixture into the eggs, then stir back into hot mixture in saucepan. Cook over low heat, stirring constantly, until thickened; remove from heat. Stir in butter and vanilla.

4. Spoon into six 1/2-cup custard cups or ramekins. Top with marshmallows. Serve warm or cold.

1 Serving: Calories 180 (Calories from Fat 40); Total Fat 4.5g (Saturated Fat 2g); Cholesterol 75mg; Sodium 95mg; Total Carbohydrate 29g (Dietary Fiber 2g; Sugars 23g); Protein 7g

% Daily Value: Vitamin A 6%; Vitamin C 0%; Calcium 10%; Iron 6%

Exchanges: 1/2 Starch, 1 Other Carbohydrate, 1/2 Skim Milk, 1 Fat

Carbohydrate Choices: 2

My mom is always looking for ways to be sure I get my calcium. This recipe is perfect—I love the chocolate and the marshmallows, mom loves the calcium!

Elizabeth H. age 8

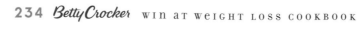

Blueberry Cheesecake Squares

Prep Time: 35 Minutes   Start to Finish: 4 Hours

16 servings

CHEESECAKE

2 cups Wheaties® cereal, crushed

1 tablespoon butter or margarine, melted

2 packages (8 oz each) reduced-fat cream cheese (Neufchâtel)

1 can (14 oz) fat-free sweetened condensed milk

1/2 cup fat-free sour cream

2 eggs or 1/2 cup fat-free egg product

1 teaspoon vanilla

BLUEBERRY TOPPING

1/4 cup sugar

1 1/2 teaspoons cornstarch

2 tablespoons water

1 tablespoon lemon juice

2 cups fresh or frozen (unsweetened) blueberries

1. Heat oven to 375°F. In 8- or 9-inch square pan, toss cereal and melted butter until cereal is well coated. Spread evenly in pan. Bake 5 to 11 minutes or until golden brown.

2. Meanwhile, in large bowl, beat cream cheese and milk with electric mixer on medium speed until smooth. Beat in sour cream, eggs and vanilla until well blended. Pour over crust.

3. Bake 35 to 40 minutes or until center is jiggly but sides are set.

4. Cool 1 hour at room temperature. Refrigerate about 2 hours or until chilled.

5. Meanwhile, in 1-quart saucepan, mix sugar and cornstarch. Stir in water and lemon juice until smooth. Add 1 cup of the blueberries. Heat to boiling over medium heat, stirring constantly. Boil about 2 minutes or until thickened; remove from heat. Stir in remaining 1 cup blueberries. Place blueberry topping in small bowl; let stand at room temperature 5 minutes. Cover and refrigerate until chilled.

6. For squares, cut cheesecake into 4 rows by 4 rows. Serve blueberry topping over cheesecake.

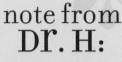

note from DR. H:

When introducing exercise, start slowly. At first, aim for 20 to 30 minutes of light to moderate activity, like walking, every other day. Gradually increase your exercise time and intensity, working up to 60 minutes every day.

1 Serving: Calories 200 (Calories from Fat 70); Total Fat 8g (Saturated Fat 5g); Cholesterol 50mg; Sodium 190mg; Total Carbohydrate 26g (Dietary Fiber 0g; Sugars 21g); Protein 6g

% Daily Value: Vitamin A 10%; Vitamin C 4%; Calcium 10%; Iron 6%

Exchanges: 1/2 Starch, 1 1/2 Other Carbohydrate, 1/2 Very Lean Meat, 1 1/2 Fat

Carbohydrate Choices: 2

Creamy Pineapple-Pecan Dessert Squares

Prep Time: 25 Minutes   **Start to Finish:** 4 Hours 30 Minutes

18 servings

3/4 cup boiling water

1 package (0.3 oz) lemon-flavored sugar-free gelatin

1 cup unsweetened pineapple juice

1 1/2 cups graham cracker crumbs

1/4 cup sugar

1/4 cup shredded coconut

1/4 cup chopped pecans

3 tablespoons butter or margarine, melted

1 package (8 oz) fat-free cream cheese

1 container (8 oz) fat-free sour cream

1/4 cup sugar

1 can (8 oz) crushed pineapple, undrained

1. In large bowl, pour boiling water over gelatin; stir about 2 minutes or until gelatin is completely dissolved. Stir in pineapple juice. Refrigerate about 30 minutes or until mixture is syrupy and just beginning to thicken.

2. Meanwhile, in 13x9-inch (3-quart) glass baking dish, toss cracker crumbs, 1/4 cup sugar, the coconut, pecans and melted butter until well mixed. Reserve 1/2 cup crumb mixture for topping. Press remaining mixture in bottom of dish.

3. In medium bowl, beat cream cheese, sour cream and 1/4 cup sugar with electric mixer on medium speed until smooth; set aside.

4. Beat gelatin mixture with electric mixer on low speed until foamy; beat on high speed until light and fluffy (mixture will look like beaten egg whites). Beat in cream cheese mixture just until mixed. Gently stir in pineapple (with liquid). Pour into crust-lined dish; smooth top. Sprinkle reserved 1/2 cup crumb mixture over top. Refrigerate about 4 hours or until set. For servings, cut into 6 rows by 3 rows.

I'm always looking for low-fat desserts that I can take to potlucks. This is a great make-and-take recipe.

Cheri O.

Creamy Pineapple-Pecan Dessert Squares

Mixed-Berry Cream Tart

Prep Time: 20 Minutes   Start to Finish: 3 Hours 30 Minutes

8 servings

note from the nutritionist:

Eat a colorful abundance of fresh fruits daily. The same pigments that give strawberries and blueberries their intense colors are thought to help prevent disease. The great thing about having fruit in dessert is that it is likely to be eaten!

2 cups sliced fresh strawberries

1/2 cup boiling water

1 package (0.3 oz) strawberry-flavored sugar-free gelatin

3 pouches (1.5 oz each) roasted almond crunchy granola bars (from 8.9-oz box)

1 package (8 oz) fat-free cream cheese

1/4 cup sugar

1/4 teaspoon almond extract

1 cup fresh blueberries

1 cup fresh raspberries

Fat-free whipped topping, if desired

1. In small bowl, crush 1 cup of the strawberries with pastry blender or fork. Reserve remaining 1 cup strawberries.

2. In medium bowl, pour boiling water over gelatin; stir about 2 minutes or until gelatin is completely dissolved. Stir crushed strawberries into gelatin. Refrigerate 20 minutes.

3. Meanwhile, leaving granola bars in pouches, crush granola bars with rolling pin. Sprinkle crushed granola in bottom of 9-inch glass pie plate, pushing crumbs up side of plate to make crust.

4. In small bowl, beat cream cheese, sugar and almond extract with electric mixer on medium-high speed until smooth. Drop by spoonfuls over crushed granola; gently spread to cover bottom of crust.

5. Gently fold blueberries, raspberries and remaining 1 cup strawberries into gelatin mixture. Spoon over cream cheese mixture. Refrigerate about 3 hours or until firm. Serve topped with whipped topping, if desired.

Never give up a chance to get up and move.

Alyson S.

1 Serving: Calories 150 (Calories from Fat 25); Total Fat 3g (Saturated Fat 0g); Cholesterol 0mg; Sodium 240mg; Total Carbohydrate 27g (Dietary Fiber 3g; Sugars 18g); Protein 7g

% Daily Value: Vitamin A 6%; Vitamin C 25%; Calcium 6%; Iron 4%

Exchanges: 1 Starch, 1/2 Fruit, 1/2 Other Carbohydrate, 1/2 Lean Meat

Carbohydrate Choices: 2

Peach and Blueberry Crisp
with Crunchy Nut Topping

Prep Time: 20 Minutes   Start to Finish: 50 Minutes

6 servings

4 medium peaches, peeled, sliced

1 cup fresh or frozen (thawed and drained) blueberries

2 tablespoons packed brown sugar

2 tablespoons orange juice

1 teaspoon ground cinnamon

1/4 teaspoon ground nutmeg

1 cup Honey Nut Clusters® cereal, slightly crushed

1/3 cup chopped pecans

1. Heat oven to 375°F. Spray 8-inch square baking dish or 11x7-inch baking dish with cooking spray.

2. In baking dish, spread peaches and blueberries. In small bowl, mix brown sugar, orange juice, cinnamon and nutmeg; drizzle over fruit.

3. Bake 15 minutes. Sprinkle with crushed cereal and pecans. Bake 10 to 15 minutes longer or until peaches are tender when pierced with a fork.

note from the nutritionist:

If you like fruit crisp with streusel topping, you'll love this recipe. Instead of the traditional butter-packed crumble, crushed cereal and nuts give this topping the same great crunch without the extra fat and calories.

1 Serving: Calories 140 (Calories from Fat 45); Total Fat 5g (Saturated Fat 0g); Cholesterol 0mg; Sodium 45mg; Total Carbohydrate 24g (Dietary Fiber 4g; Sugars 16g); Protein 2g

% Daily Value: Vitamin A 2%; Vitamin C 8%; Calcium 2%; Iron 8%

Exchanges: 1/2 Starch, 1 Fruit, 1 Fat

Carbohydrate Choices: 1 1/2

family menus

To start on a healthy eating path, here is a week's worth of meal suggestions. You can think of them as ideas for meals and snacks that center around moderate calories and fat and higher fiber.

If you are trying to lose weight, you will want to decrease your calorie and fat intake and increase your activity level. These daily menus vary from about 1,750 to 1,945 calories and 39 to 62.5 grams of total fat.

Children's nutrient requirements vary by age; they may need more or less of these nutrients depending on their age and activity level. Check with a health professional for more information.

You can mix and match meals from different days to add variety and tailor your plan to your family's needs. Do keep track of calories and fat to make sure you're not eating too much or too little. Here's to your family's good health!

Based on your individual calorie needs, shoot for these daily goals:

Total fat—30 percent or less of total calories

Saturated fat—10 percent or less of total calories

Dietary cholesterol—300 milligrams or less per day

Dietary fiber—25 grams or more per day

MONDAY

Breakfast
1 serving Cheerios® cereal
1 cup fat-free (skim) milk
1 medium banana or 1/2 cup blueberries
1 cup coffee or herbal tea
CALORIES 310 · TOTAL FAT 3G

Lunch
1 serving Southwest Pork Soup (page 113)
1 Parmesan-Sesame Breadstick (page 82) or 1 slice
    whole wheat bread or 1 small dinner roll or
    4 reduced-fat wheat crackers
1 teaspoon squeeze or soft tub margarine
Carrot and celery sticks
2 tablespoons reduced-fat vegetable or ranch dip
1 medium nectarine
1 cup water
CALORIES 610 · TOTAL FAT 23G

Dinner
1 serving Halibut with Potato Succotash (page 144)
1 serving Dilled Cucumber-Tomato Salad (page 194) or
    1 cup steamed green beans
1 small whole-grain dinner roll
1 teaspoon squeeze or soft tub margarine
1 serving Blueberry Cake Bars (page 224)
1 cup fat-free (skim) milk
CALORIES 640 · TOTAL FAT 18G

Snack
(can be eaten any time during the day)
1 medium orange or tangerine
6 ounces low-fat yogurt or 1/2 cup sugar-free fat-free
    chocolate pudding made with fat-free (skim) milk
2 tablespoons fat-free whipped topping
CALORIES 250 · TOTAL FAT 2G

DAILY TOTAL: CALORIES 1810 · TOTAL FAT 46G
CARBOHYDRATE 268G · PROTEIN 106G · FIBER 32G

TUESDAY

Breakfast
1 Sunny Lemon-Raspberry Muffin (page 51)
1 cup fat-free (skim) milk
1 medium orange
CALORIES 340 · TOTAL FAT 7G

Lunch
1 serving Chicken and Veggies Stir-Fry (page 102)
1 cup grapes
1/2 cup bell pepper strips or cucumber slices
1 cup fat-free (skim) milk
CALORIES 660 · TOTAL FAT 10G

Dinner
1 serving Skillet Beef, Veggies and Brown Rice (page 107)
1 serving Mixed-Fruit Salad (page 199) or mixed-greens salad with 2 tablespoons reduced-fat Caesar (or other flavor) dressing
1 Double Chocolate–Peanut Butter Cupcake (page 232)
1 cup fat-free (skim) milk
CALORIES 580 · TOTAL FAT 12G

Snack
(can be eaten any time during the day)
1 serving Sugar 'n Spice Snack (page 70)
1 medium apple
CALORIES 310 · TOTAL FAT 10G

DAILY TOTALS: CALORIES 1890 · TOTAL FAT 39G
CARBOHYDRATE 299G · PROTEIN 98G · FIBER 25G

WEDNESDAY

Breakfast
1 serving Blueberry Breakfast Cereal Bread (page 53)
1/2 cup sliced strawberries
1 cup fat-free yogurt (any flavor)
CALORIES 400 · TOTAL FAT 3G

Lunch
1 serving Caesar Shrimp Salad (page 190)
1 slice whole-grain bread or 1 small dinner roll
1 teaspoon squeeze or soft tub margarine
1/2 cup baby-cut carrots, corn or peas
1/2 cup pineapple chunks
CALORIES 650 · TOTAL FAT 14G

Dinner
1 serving Chicken and Noodles Skillet (page 98)
1 serving Easy Bean Salad (page 196)
1 Raspberry-Chocolate Bar (page 226)
1 cup fat-free (skim) milk
CALORIES 590 · TOTAL FAT 17G

Snack
(can be eaten any time during the day)
1/4 cup reduced-fat cottage cheese
1/4 cup sunflower nuts
or
1/2 cup reduced-fat frozen yogurt or ice cream with
1 tablespoon fat-free chocolate fudge topping
CALORIES 260 · TOTAL FAT 19G

DAILY TOTAL: CALORIES 1900 · TOTAL FAT 53G
CARBOHYDRATE 257G · PROTEIN 108G · FIBER 27G

THURSDAY

Breakfast
1 serving Bacon, Cheese and Tomato Strata (page 54)
2 slices whole wheat bread, toasted
2 teaspoons jam or jelly
1/2 cup cranberry juice
CALORIES 410 · TOTAL FAT 9G

Lunch
1 serving Parmesan Rice and Peas with Bacon (page 188)
1 cup baby-cut carrots
1 medium banana
1 cup fat-free (skim) milk
CALORIES 410 · TOTAL FAT 6G

Dinner
1 serving Pork Chops with Cheesy Corn Bread Stuffing
    (page 136)
1 cup steamed broccoli with lemon
1 serving Mixed-Berry Cream Tart (page 238)
CALORIES 650 · TOTAL FAT 19G

Snack
(can be eaten any time during the day)
1 serving Fruit and Nut Bread with Browned Butter Glaze
    (page 83) or
2 Sassy Cinnamon Cookies (page 229)
1 cup fat-free (skim) milk
CALORIES 280 · TOTAL FAT 8G

DAILY TOTALS: CALORIES 1750 · TOTAL FAT 42G
CARBOHYDRATE 259G · PROTEIN 98G · FIBER 25G

FRIDAY

Breakfast
1 serving Creamy Peachsicle Smoothie (page 66)
1 whole wheat English muffin
2 teaspoons peanut butter
CALORIES 430 · TOTAL FAT 7G

Lunch
1 serving Chicken and Berry Salad (page 175)
1 serving Texas Coleslaw (page 197)
1 medium apple
1 cup fat-free (skim) milk
CALORIES 490 · TOTAL FAT 15G

Dinner
1 serving Bean and Cheese Skillet Supper (page 117)
1 serving Carrots with Parsley Butter (page 209)
1 serving Peach and Blueberry Crisp with Crunchy Nut
    Topping (page 239)
CALORIES 570 · TOTAL FAT 16G

Snack
(can be eaten any time during the day)
1 serving Peanut Butter Snack Bars (page 71) or Cheesy
    Italian Tomato Toasts (page 76)
1 cup chocolate fat-free (skim) milk
CALORIES 340 · TOTAL FAT 7G

DAILY TOTAL: CALORIES 1830 · TOTAL FAT 45G
CARBOHYDRATE 298G · PROTEIN 85G · FIBER 40G

SATURDAY

Breakfast
1 serving Cinnamon-Pear Oatmeal with Toasted Walnuts
  (page 63)
1/2 cup cherries or 1 medium banana
1 serving hot herbal tea or coffee
CALORIES 410 · TOTAL FAT 10G

Lunch
1 serving Beef and Cheese Foldover Sandwiches
  (page 178)
1 serving Marinated Carrot Salad (page 210) or
  Wiggly Jiggly Fruit Salad (page 200)
1 cup fat-free (skim) milk
CALORIES 560 · TOTAL FAT 23G

Dinner
1 serving Corn Flake–Crusted Fish Fillets (page 142)
1 serving Peanutty Pear Salad (page 198)
1 serving Streusel-Topped Squash (page 208)
1 cup raw or cooked bell pepper strips
1 cup fat-free (skim) milk
CALORIES 72 · TOTAL FAT 25G

Snack
(can be eaten any time during the day)
1 medium pear
3 cups light popcorn
1 cup fat-free (skim) milk
CALORIES 250 · TOTAL FAT 4.5G
DAILY TOTAL:

**DAILY TOTALS: CALORIES 1945 · TOTAL FAT 62.5G
CARBOHYDRATE 266G · PROTEIN 98G · FIBER 27G**

SUNDAY

Breakfast
1 serving Crunchy Oven French Toast (page 49)
2 tablespoons maple-flavor syrup or preserves
1 cup fat-free (skim) milk
1 cup fresh raspberries or blueberries
CALORIES 340 · TOTAL FAT 4G

Lunch
1 serving Beef-Barley Soup (page 123)
6 whole-grain crackers with 1 to 2 ounces mozzarella cheese
1 medium hard roll
1 teaspoon squeeze or soft tub margarine
1 cup cherry tomatoes or grape tomatoes
1 cup fat-free (skim) milk
CALORIES 730 · TOTAL FAT 20G

Dinner
1 serving Wild Rice–Turkey Pot Pie (page 151)
1 serving Dilly Beans (page 90)
1 serving Blueberry Cheesecake Squares (page 235)
1 cup hot herbal tea or coffee
CALORIES   620 · TOTAL FAT 21G

Snack
(can be eaten any time during the day)
1 serving Three-Cheese and Bacon Spread (page 80) with
  6 whole wheat crackers or 1 whole-grain granola bar
1/2 cup apple juice or apple cider
CALORIES 150 · TOTAL FAT 2.5G

**DAILY TOTALS: CALORIES 1840 · TOTAL FAT 47.5G
CARBOHYDRATE 267G · PROTEIN 107G · FIBER 26G**

resources

Your health care professional is your first resource for information about good health and nutrition for the whole family. Here are some additional resources you may find helpful.

The Step Diet—This book tells you what you really need to know to lose weight and keep it off forever. It comes with a pedometer and lifetime physical activity plan. www.stepdietbook.com.

The American Academy of Pediatrics—An authoritative source for information on a wide range of children's health topics, including childhood overweight and obesity. Visit its Web site at www.aap.org, or call 847-434-4000.

The American Association for the Child's Right to Play—This action group focuses on promoting play as "a fundamental right for all humans," and is an advocate for preserving recess in schools. Find tips for organizing a "Play Day" in your community or school, as well as links to resources, games and activities for all ages. www.ipausa.org.

The American Dietetic Association—The ADA can provide customized answers to your questions about nutrition. Call them at 800-366-1655 to obtain a referral to a registered dietitian in your area. You can also listen to recorded messages about food and nutrition. Check out the American Dietetic Association's Web site at www.eatright.org.

America on the Move—A national campaign to help Americans take small steps to eat less and move more, based on a pioneering program developed by the University of Colorado Health Sciences Center. Find tips for making small lifestyle changes that make a big difference, such as eating 100 fewer calories and walking 2,000 additional steps daily. You can also register individually or as a group to help get your community or workplace "on the move." 800-807-0077, or www.americaonthemove.org.

The National Association of Anorexia Nervosa and Associated Disorders (ANAD)—A helpful source for information, hotline counseling, treatment options and referrals, support groups and more. Call the hotline at 847-831-3438; Web site: www.anad.org.

The National Weight Control Registry—This online registry documents the successes and stories of over 5,000 successful "losers" who have lost at least 30 pounds and kept the weight off for over a year. Log on for inspiration, research findings about registry participants, or to sign up yourself. www.nwcr.ws; 800-606-NWCR (6927).

President's Council on Physical Fitness and Sports—This government-funded organization aims to encourage Americans of all ages to become more active. It is best known for the President's Challenge awards—fitness challenges for schools, camps and clubs. For more information, call 202-690-9000, or log on at www.fitness.gov.

Putting Family First—This citizens' group focuses on empowering people and communities to support families. Its Web site has tips for creating more family time by setting limits on outside activities, television and other electronic media, as well as guidelines for making family dinners a priority. The organization also founded Family Day, the fourth Monday in September, when families are encouraged to celebrate a meal together at home. www.puttingfamilyfirst.org.

Shape Up America—This Web site provides lots of information about healthy eating, exercise and sensible weight management for all ages. There's a free BMI calculator for both adults and children, portion control quizzes and more. www.shapeupamerica.org.

STEP EQUIVALENTS FOR KIDS

Encouraging healthy eating and physical activity in childhood can promote healthy lifestyle behaviors in children that will last a lifetime. The key principles mentioned in this book—managing portions so as not to overeat, choosing lower-calorie snacks and meals and walking or moving more—work very well for kids, too.

Kids with actively growing bodies actually need a lot of physical activity, even more than adults, so get them moving. Kids naturally like to move and feel most comfortable in an environment where they can play and have fun, inside and outside. Every minute that they are up, moving and playing is time well spent. Trying different activities is worth doing, both for enjoyment and for self-esteem, as well as using different muscles.

Have fun moving with your kids. Play with them at a playground or a park. Walk with them, toss the baseball or football, kick a soccer ball or run after them at the playground. And plan active trips, like camping or beach vacations. While 10,000–12,000 steps per day may be adequate for adults, kids' steps (or an equivalent activity) need to be closer to 15,000 or more. The following step equivalents are estimated for 10-year-old boys and girls, but teens need about the same amount of activity as what's listed in the table below.

Activity	Step Equivalent (per Minute)
Walking	120
Baseball or Softball	120
Basketball	200
Canoeing	80
Dancing	120
Football	160
Hockey (field or ice)	200
Ice Skating	160
Jumping rope	280
Lacrosse	200
Playing ping pong	120
Rollerblading	200
Shopping	80
Sledding	110
Snowboarding	160
Soccer	200
Swimming	160
Tennis	200
Volleyball	120

THE *STEP DIET* BOOK

Are you one of the millions who have dieted for months, lost weight only to gradually gain it back in a couple of months?

Are you looking for a way to lose weight, keep it off forever and live healthier?

The Step Diet is for you!

The authors of the *Step Diet* book based the program on sound scientific research. The program is easy to follow and allows you to lose weight, and most importantly, keep it off for good! Most diets ultimately fail because they provide a temporary solution, not a permanent way to live your life at a lower weight. There is a way to lose weight without giving those excess pounds a round-trip ticket. The Step Diet is based on research conducted by James Hill, Ph.D., John Peters, Ph.D., and Bonnie Jortberg, M.S., R.D. and many other researchers. They studied not just how to lose weight but how to make small, permanent changes in your lifestyle to keep that weight off forever. The Step Diet is people-tested and easy to follow! The *Step Diet* book comes with a step counter and all the information you need to begin your Step Diet program.

It's easy to get started—all you have to do is put one foot in front of the other!

How does the Step Diet work to help you lose weight and keep it off forever?

To lose weight successfully you need to reduce the calories you consume in relation to the energy your body burns through your resting metabolism and your physical activity. That is not new. What is new is that the Step Diet does not focus on counting calories or eating particular foods. The Step Diet shows you a simple way to reduce your energy intake to lose weight and, most importantly, it shows you a simple way to compensate for the drop in your metabolism that occurs when you lose weight.

The Step Diet shows you how to increase the number of steps you walk to continue to burn the energy necessary to maintain your weight loss for life. The secret of the Step Diet is that it doesn't focus on food **or** physical activity as most di-

ets do, but rather on **energy balance**—the balance between food and activity. You can achieve this with two simple tools, a bathroom scale and the **Step Counter** that comes with this book. If you can maintain energy balance at your desired weight you will succeed at long-term weight maintenance. The Step Diet makes this easy by focusing on these steps:

BodySteps—The energy burned through your body's resting metabolism, converted into steps.

LifeSteps—The energy burned through physical activity or steps measured by the Step Counter included with the book.

MegaSteps—The total energy your body burns. (BodySteps + LifeSteps = MegaSteps)

The *Principles of the Step Diet Book* and *Step Diet Stages of Weight Loss* detail how to lose weight by un-supersizing your food portions and by gradually increasing the number of steps you walk throughout the day to increase your energy expenditure. Once you have lost the weight, the *Step Diet* book shows you how to manage and maintain your weight loss by helping you determine how many daily steps you need to take to balance the food you eat.

Principles of the *Step Diet* book:

1. Maintain the proper energy balance.

2. Small changes drive success.

3. Start with physical activity.

4. Anticipate success, but not instantly.

5. The maintenance of weight loss is more important than the speed or amount of weight loss.

america on the move

Inspiring Americans to Achieve Healthier Lifestyles

America On the Move is a national initiative dedicated to helping individuals and communities across our nation make positive changes to improve health and quality of life. By focusing on individuals and communities AOM strives to support healthy eating and active living habits in our society. AOM:

Inspires Americans to engage in fun, simple ways to become more active and eat more healthfully to achieve and maintain a healthy weight.

Creates and supports an integrated grassroots network of state affiliates to build communities that support individual behavior changes.

Encourages public and private partnerships at the national, state and local level to build the capacity, reach and support needed for individual and community behavior change.

The Challenge

The eating and physical activity patterns of most Americans have made us the most overweight nation in the world. More than 60 percent of American adults do not get the recommended 30 minutes of physical activity a day; 25 percent of American adults are not physically active at all. More than 120 million Americans—64.5 percent of the adult population—are overweight; nearly 59 million, or 31 percent, are obese. The average American adult is gaining one to three pounds each year, and some people gain even more.

Individual Change

It's all about energy balance! We can stop weight gain by creating a balance between the amount of energy burned and the amount of food consumed throughout a normal day. The message is simple: move more and eat less. Making these two small changes daily is all it takes. By walking an extra 2,000 steps (the equivalent of about one mile) and eating only 100 fewer calories each day, individuals can prevent weight gain and begin to see big results.

Community Change

To be successful at creating sustainable individual behavior change, AOM must focus on the larger environment and create communities that support healthy eating and active living. By reaching individuals where they live, work, learn and play, communities can make a difference. AOM encourages stakeholders from both the public and private sectors to be part of the solution!

Our Philosophy and Applied Approach

America On the Move and our partners will:

Address the problem of unhealthy lifestyles in America in a positive and proactive way.

Respect the dignity of all individuals by inspiring healthy choices rather than emphasizing weight and appearance.

Include the imagination, talents and commitment of multiple stakeholders—public and private sectors will come together to address the health crisis facing our nation.

Empower individuals and communities to make informed choices regarding healthful eating and active living through effective communication guided by sound, evidence-based information.

Foster an understanding of the connection between daily physical activity/eating behavior choices and their impact on health.

Increase the likelihood that individuals will adopt healthy behaviors by encouraging them to start from where they are and incorporate small changes into their busy daily routines, building confidence for continued change efforts.

Assure easy access for all to America On the Move™ resources and systems.

HeLPFUL NUTRITION anD COOKING information

Nutrition Guidelines

We provide nutrition information for each recipe that includes calories, fat, cholesterol, sodium, carbohydrate, fiber and protein. Individual food choices can be based on this information.

Recommended intake for a daily diet of 2,000 calories as set by the Food and Drug Administration

Total Fat	Less than 65g
Saturated Fat	Less than 20g
Cholesterol	Less than 300mg
Sodium	Less than 2,400mg
Total Carbohydrate	300g
Dietary Fiber	25g

Criteria Used for Calculating Nutrition Information

- The first ingredient was used wherever a choice is given (such as 1/3 cup sour cream or plain yogurt).

- The first ingredient amount was used wherever a range is given (such as 3- to 3 1/2-pound cut-up broiler-fryer chicken).

- The first serving number was used wherever a range is given (such as 4 to 6 servings).

- "If desired" ingredients and recipe variations were not included (such as sprinkle with brown sugar, if desired).

- Only the amount of a marinade or frying oil that is estimated to be absorbed by the food during preparation or cooking was calculated.

Ingredients Used in Recipe Testing and Nutrition Calculations

- Ingredients used for testing represent those that the majority of consumers use in their homes: large eggs, skim milk, 80%-lean ground beef, canned ready-to-use chicken broth and vegetable oil spread containing not less than 65 percent fat.

- Fat-free, low-fat or low-sodium products were not used, unless otherwise indicated.

- Solid vegetable shortening (not butter, margarine, nonstick cooking sprays or vegetable oil spread, as they can cause sticking problems) was used to grease pans, unless otherwise indicated.

Equipment Used in Recipe Testing

We use equipment for testing that the majority of consumers use in their homes. If a specific piece of equipment (such as a wire whisk) is necessary for recipe success, it is listed in the recipe.

- Cookware and bakeware without nonstick coatings were used, unless otherwise indicated.

- No dark-colored, black or insulated bakeware was used.

- When a pan is specified in a recipe, a metal pan was used; a baking dish or pie plate means ovenproof glass was used.

- An electric hand mixer was used for mixing only when mixer speeds are specified in the recipe directions. When a mixer speed is not given, a spoon or fork was used.

Cooking Terms Glossary

Beat: Mix ingredients vigorously with spoon, fork, wire whisk, hand beater or electric mixer until smooth and uniform.

Boil: Heat liquid until bubbles rise continuously and break on the surface and steam is given off. For rolling boil, the bubbles form rapidly.

Chop: Cut into coarse or fine irregular pieces with a knife, food chopper, blender or food processor.

Cube: Cut into squares 1/2 inch or larger.

Dice: Cut into squares smaller than 1/2 inch.

Grate: Cut into tiny particles using small rough holes of grater (citrus peel or chocolate).

Grease: Rub the inside surface of a pan with shortening, using pastry brush, piece of waxed paper or paper towel, to prevent food from sticking during baking (as for some casseroles).

Julienne: Cut into thin, matchlike strips, using knife or food processor (vegetables, fruits, meats).

Mix: Combine ingredients in any way that distributes them evenly.

Sauté: Cook foods in hot oil or margarine over medium-high heat with frequent tossing and turning motion.

Shred: Cut into long thin pieces by rubbing food across the holes of a shredder, as for cheese, or by using a knife to slice very thinly, as for cabbage.

Simmer: Cook in liquid just below the boiling point on top of the stove; usually after reducing heat from a boil. Bubbles will rise slowly and break just below the surface.

Stir: Mix ingredients until uniform consistency. Stir once in a while for stirring occasionally, often for stirring frequently and continuously for stirring constantly.

Toss: Tumble ingredients (such as green salad) lightly with a lifting motion, usually to coat evenly or mix with another food.

metric conversion guide

VOLUME

U.S. Units	Canadian Metric	Australian Metric
1/4 teaspoon	1 mL	1 ml
1/2 teaspoon	2 mL	2 ml
1 teaspoon	5 mL	5 ml
1 tablespoon	15 mL	20 ml
1/4 cup	50 mL	60 ml
1/3 cup	75 mL	80 ml
1/2 cup	125 mL	125 ml
2/3 cup	150 mL	170 ml
3/4 cup	175 mL	190 ml
1 cup	250 mL	250 ml
1 quart	1 liter	1 liter
1 1/2 quarts	1.5 liters	1.5 liters
2 quarts	2 liters	2 liters
2 1/2 quarts	2.5 liters	2.5 liters
3 quarts	3 liters	3 liters
4 quarts	4 liters	4 liters

WEIGHT

U.S. Units	Canadian Metric	Australian Metric
1 ounce	30 grams	30 grams
2 ounces	55 grams	60 grams
3 ounces	85 grams	90 grams
4 ounces (1/4 pound)	115 grams	125 grams
8 ounces (1/2 pound)	225 grams	225 grams
16 ounces (1 pound)	455 grams	500 grams
1 pound	455 grams	1/2 kilogram

MEASUREMENTS

Inches	Centimeters
1	2.5
2	5.0
3	7.5
4	10.0
5	12.5
6	15.0
7	17.5
8	20.5
9	23.0
10	25.5
11	28.0
12	30.5
13	33.0

TEMPERATURES

Fahrenheit	Celsius
32°	0°
212°	100°
250°	120°
275°	140°
300°	150°
325°	160°
350°	180°
375°	190°
400°	200°
425°	220°
450°	230°
475°	240°
500°	260°

Index

Note: *Italicized* page references indicate photographs and illustrations.